1,001
KOSHER
JOKES

Jonah
Press

1,001 KOSHER JOKES

For Clean Fun

Doron Kornbluth

Published by Jonah Press
A division of Mosaica Press, Inc.

Printed in Bulgaria

TABLE OF CONTENTS

SPORTS JOKES

1   I was wondering why the baseball was getting bigger. Then it hit me.

2   People tell me I take mini golf too seriously, but my caddy disagrees.

3   Why does a pitcher raise one leg when he throws the ball? If he raised them both, he'd fall down.

4   Where do they keep the largest diamond in NYC? Yankee Stadium.

5   A man leaves home, makes three left turns, and is on his way back home when he notices two men in masks waiting for him. They're the catcher and umpire.

6 What goes all the way around the baseball field but never moves? The fence.

7 What's the difference between a pickpocket and an umpire? One steals watches and one watches steals.

8 What did the baseball glove say to the ball? Catch ya' later!

9 Where do catchers sit at lunch? Behind the plate.

10 Why is Yankee Stadium the coolest place to be? It's full of fans.

11 What are the rules for zebra baseball? Three stripes and you're out.

12 Why are umpires always overweight? It's their job to clean their plates.

13 What's a baseball player to do when his eyesight starts to fail him? He takes a job as an umpire.

14 Where do you keep your mitt while driving? In the glove compartment.

15   Which baseball player holds water? The pitcher.

16   Why are baseball games at night? The bats sleep during the day.

17   What is the difference between Yankee fans and dentists? One roots for the yanks, and the other yanks for the roots.

18   What has eighteen legs and catches flies? A baseball team.

19   How do baseball players keep in touch? They touch base every once in a while.

20   Why are basketball players such messy eaters? They're always dribbling.

21   Why can't basketball players go on vacation? They aren't allowed to travel.

22   Which fast food chain is most likely to win a basketball tournament? Dunkin' Donuts.

23   Why was the basketball player sitting on the sidelines drawing chickens? Coach told her to learn how to draw fouls.

24   Why do basketball players like cookies?
It's just another excuse to dunk.

25   Why did the fish refuse to play basketball?
He was afraid of the net.

26   Why are frogs so good at basketball?
They always make the jump shots.

27   What kind of tea do football players drink?
Penal-tea.

28   Why couldn't the All-Star football player listen
to any music? He broke all the records.

29   How are scrambled eggs and football teams
the same? They've both been beaten.

30   What's harder to catch the faster you run?
Your breath.

31   Why couldn't the defensive end pass any
of his tests? He was a tackling dummy.

32   What do you get when you cross a quarterback
with a carpet? A throw rug.

33   I watched hockey before it was cool.
You might call it swimming.

34   What do a hockey player and a magician have
in common? They both do hat tricks.

35   Where does most of a hockey player's salary
come from? The tooth fairy.

36   What do you give a hockey player when
he demands to be paid? A check.

37   Hockey players are like goldfish. Just tap on the
glass to get their attention.

38   My friend and I visited Canada together for the
first time. We went to a fight, and a hockey
game broke out.

39   Why are hockey players so good at making
friends? They're quick to break the ice.

40   How many teeth does a hockey player have?
Don't you mean tooth?

41   Why are soccer players excellent at math?
They know how to use their heads.

42   Two soccer teams play a game against each other. The home team wins, but not a single man from either team scored a goal. How can this be? They were women's teams.

43   Which goalie can jump higher than the crossbars? All of them. Crossbars can't jump.

44   Why can't you play soccer in the jungle? There are too many cheetahs.

45   Which soccer player wears the biggest cleats? The one with the biggest feet.

46   What did the coach say to the broken vending machine? I want my quarter back!

47   When is a baseball player like a spider? When he catches a fly!

48   What kinds of stories do basketball players tell? Tall tales!

49   How is a baseball team similar to a pancake? They both need a good batter!

50   Why did the golfer wear two pairs of pants? In case he got a hole in one!

LAWYER JOKES

51   What's the difference between a good lawyer and a bad lawyer? A bad lawyer might let a case drag on for several years. A good lawyer knows how to make it last even longer.

52   What's the difference between a lawyer and a jellyfish? One is a spineless, poisonous blob. The other is a form of sea life.

53   A fifty-year-old lawyer who had been practicing since he was twenty-five passed away and arrived Upstairs for judgment. The lawyer said to the angel, "There must be some mistake! I'm only fifty years old, that's far too young to die!" The angel frowned and consulted his book. "That's funny, when we add up your billing records, we calculated that you should be at least eighty-three by now!"

54 What separates witnesses from the lowest form of life on earth? The wooden partitions around the witness stand.

55 A young lawyer, defending a businessman in a lawsuit, feared he was losing the case and asked his senior partner if he should send a box of cigars to the judge to curry favor. The senior partner was horrified. "The judge is one of the most honest and honorable people I've ever met," he said. "If you do that, I guarantee you'll lose the case—automatically!" Eventually, the judge ruled for the young lawyer. "Aren't you glad you didn't send those cigars?" the senior partner asked. "Oh, I did send them," the younger lawyer replied. "I just enclosed my opponent's business card with them."

56 How many lawyer jokes are there, anyway? Only three. The rest are true.

57 A new client had just come in to see a famous lawyer. "Can you tell me how much you charge?" asked the client. "Of course," the lawyer replied, "I charge $200 to answer three questions!" "Well, that's a bit steep, isn't it?" remarked the client. "Yes, it is," said the lawyer. "And what's your third question?"

58 What's wrong with lawyer jokes? Lawyers don't think they're funny, and nobody else thinks they're jokes.

59 How do you tell if a lawyer is lying? His lips are moving.

60 Why do they bury lawyers one hundred feet into the ground? Because down deep, they're good people.

61 What do lawyers wear to court? Lawsuits!

62 You need a new lawyer when...
- When the prosecutors see who your lawyer is, they high-five each other.
- He picks the jury by playing "duck-duck-goose."
- During the trial, you catch him playing his Gameboy.
- A prison guard is shaving your head.
- Just before trial starts, he whispers, "The judge is the one with the little hammer, right?"
- Just before he says, "Your Honor," he makes those little quotation marks in the air with his fingers.

- The sign in front of his law office reads "Practicing Law Since 2:25 PM."
- Whenever his objection is overruled, he tells the judge, "Whatever."

63 A big shot city lawyer and an old country farmer got into a car wreck. They both got out of their cars to survey the damage. After looking over the lawyer in his $1,000 suit, the farmer walked back to his car, got out a bottle, and brought it back. He handed it to the lawyer, and said, "Here, you look pretty shaken up. I think you ought to take a nip of this. It'll steady your nerves." The lawyer did. The farmer said, "You still look a little bit pale. How about another?" The lawyer took another swallow. At the urging of the farmer, he took another, and another, and another. Finally, the lawyer said he was feeling pretty good and asked the farmer if he didn't think that he ought to have a little nip too. "Not me," the farmer replied. "I'm waiting for the state trooper."

64 A restaurant was so sure that its chef was the strongest man in the world that it offered $1,000 to anyone who could beat him in one task. The chef squeezed a lemon until all the juice ran out. Anyone who could get a drop of juice out of it after that was done would win the $1,000. Many strong people had tried and failed. One day a scrawny man came into the restaurant wearing thick glasses and a polyester suit. He squeaked, "I'd like to try the bet." After the laughter died down, the chef grabbed a lemon and squeezed away. Then he handed the rind to the man, who to everyone's amazement, squeezed six drops into the glass. Stunned, the chef paid up, and then asked the man, "What do you do for a living? Are you a lumberjack? A weight lifter?" "Nope," the man replied. "I'm an attorney for the IRS."

65   Three lawyers and three accountants got on the train in New York to go to a convention in DC. The three accountants bought a ticket each, but the three lawyers bought only one ticket between them. The accountants commented on the illegality of their action, but the lawyers said, "Trust us—we're lawyers." When the conductor entered the end of the car to collect the tickets, the three lawyers got up and all went into the bathroom together. When the conductor knocked on the bathroom door, a hand shot out with the one ticket, which the conductor duly cancelled. On returning to their seats, the three accountants expressed admiration for such a clever trick. "Well," they said modestly, "we ARE lawyers." After the convention they all entered Union Station for the return trip home to New York. This time the accountants bought one ticket between them, while the lawyers did not buy any tickets at all. The accountants were amazed and said so. "Trust us," the three said, "we're lawyers." When the conductor arrived, the three accountants quickly jumped up and went into the bathroom. As soon as the door closed, the three lawyers got up and headed for the adjoining bathroom. As the last lawyer went by the accountants' bathroom, he knocked on the door. A hand shot out with the ticket, which the lawyer quickly grabbed before entering the other bathroom.

66   Lawyers think they have found solid grounds for an appeal of Mr. Smith's murder conviction: They discovered that he still has a lot of money.

67   Did you hear that the Post Office just recalled their latest stamps? They had pictures of lawyers on them...and people couldn't figure out which side to spit on.

68   Mr. Wilson was the chairman of the United Way, which had never received a donation from the most successful lawyer in town. He called on the attorney in an attempt to persuade him to mend his ways. "Our research shows that you made a profit of over $600,000 last year, and yet you have not given a dime to the community charities! What do you have to say for yourself?" The lawyer replied, "Did your research also show that my mother is dying after a long illness and has medical bills that are several times her annual income? Do you know about my brother, the disabled veteran, who is blind and in a wheelchair? Do you know about my sister, whose husband died in a traffic accident, leaving her penniless with three children?" Sheepishly, the charity solicitor admitted that he had no knowledge of any of this. "Well, since I don't give any money to them, why should I give any to you?"

69 A lawyer was filling out a job application when he came to the question, "Have you ever been arrested?" He answered, "No." The next question, intended for people who had answered in the affirmative to the last one, was "Why?" The lawyer answered it anyway: "Never got caught."

70 A defending attorney was cross-examining a coroner. The attorney asked, "Before you signed the death certificate, had you taken the man's pulse?" "No," the coroner replied. The attorney then asked, "Did you listen for a heartbeat?" The coroner said, "No." "Did you check for breathing?" asked the attorney. Again, the coroner replied, "No." The attorney asked, "So when you signed the death certificate, you had not taken any steps to make sure the man was dead, had you?" The coroner, now tired of the browbeating, said, "Well, let me put it this way. The man's brain was sitting in a jar on my desk, but for all I know, he could be out there practicing law somewhere."

71   Real lawyers' questions from official court records:

- Now, Doctor, isn't it true that when a person dies in his sleep, in most cases he just passes quietly away and doesn't know anything about it until the next morning?
- Was it you or your brother who was killed in the war?
- The youngest son, the twenty-year-old, how old is he?
- Do you have any children or anything of that kind?
- Were you present in court this morning when you were sworn in?
- Now, Mrs. Johnson, how was your first marriage terminated?
  By death.
  And by whose death was it terminated?

- She had three children, right?
  Yes.
  How many were boys?
  None.
  Were there girls?
- You don't know what it was, and you didn't know what it looked like, but can you describe it?
- You say that the stairs went down to the basement?
  Yes.
  And these stairs, did they go up also?
- Have you lived in this town all your life?
  Not yet.

72 The old man was critically ill. Feeling that death was near, he called his lawyer.
"I want to become a lawyer. How much is it for that express degree you told me about?"
"It's $50,000," the lawyer said, "but why? You'll be dead soon—why do you want to become a lawyer?" "That's my business! Get me the course!" Four days later, the old man got his law degree. His lawyer was at his bedside, making sure his bill would be paid. Suddenly the old man was racked with fits of coughing, and it was clear that this would be the end. Still curious, the lawyer leaned over and said, "Please, before it's too late, tell me why you

wanted to get a law degree so badly before you died." In a faint whisper, as he breathed his last, the old man said: "One less lawyer."

73   The lawyer's son wanted to follow in his father's footsteps, so he went to law school. He graduated with honors and then went home to join his father's firm. At the end of his first day at work, he rushed into his father's office and said, "Father, Father, in one day I broke the accident case that you've been working on for ten years!" His father responded: "You fool, we lived on the funding of that case for ten years!"

74   A lawyer was interrogating a witness at the stand. The witness was a punk from the streets. "You've got a lot of intelligence for someone of your background," the lawyer sneered.
"I'd return the compliment if I wasn't under oath," the punk replied.

75   What's the difference between a lawyer and a catfish? One's an ugly bottom-feeder and the other is a fish.

76   What's the difference between God and a lawyer? God doesn't think He's a lawyer.

77   What's the difference between a lawyer and a leech? A leech quits sucking your blood after you die.

78   What is a criminal lawyer? Redundant.

79   What are lawyers good for? They make used car salesmen look good.

80   What did the lawyer name his daughter? Sue. And his son? Bill.

81   What do you call a person who assists a criminal in breaking the law before the criminal gets arrested? An accomplice. What do you call a person who assists a criminal in breaking the law after the criminal gets arrested? A lawyer.

82   Why are lawyers never attacked by sharks? Professional courtesy.

83   How many lawyers does it take to screw in a light bulb? Just one; he holds it still and the whole world revolves around him.

84   Why does California have the most lawyers, and New Jersey, the most toxic waste dumps? New Jersey got first pick.

85   It was so cold last winter...(How cold was it?)...that I saw a lawyer with his hands in his *own* pockets.

86   A tourist wanders into a back-alley antique shop in San Francisco's Chinatown. Picking through the objects on display, he discovers a detailed life-sized bronze sculpture of a rat. The sculpture is so interesting and unique that he picks it up and asks the shop owner what it costs. "Twelve dollars for the rat, sir," says the shop owner, "and a thousand dollars more for the story behind it." "You can keep the story, old man," he replies, "but I'll take the rat." The transaction complete, the tourist leaves the store with the bronze rat under his arm. As he crosses the street in front of the store, two live rats emerge from a sewer drain and fall into step behind him. Nervously looking over his shoulder, he begins to walk faster, but every time he passes another sewer drain, more rats come out and follow him. By the time he's walked two blocks, at least a hundred rats are at his heels, and people begin to point and shout. He walks even faster, and soon breaks into a trot as multitudes of rats swarm from sewers, basements, vacant lots, and abandoned cars. Rats by the thousands are at his heels, and as he sees the waterfront at the bottom of the hill, he panics and starts to run full tilt. No matter how fast he runs, the rats keep up, squealing hideously, now not just thousands but millions, so that by the time he comes rushing up to the water's edge, a trail of rats twelve city blocks long is behind him. Making a mighty leap, he jumps up onto a light post, grasping it with one arm while he hurls the bronze rat into San Francisco Bay with the other, as far as he can heave it. Pulling his legs up and clinging to the light post, he watches in amazement as the seething tide of rats surges over the breakwater into the sea, where they drown. Shaken and mumbling, he makes his way back to the antique shop. "Ah, so you've come back for the rest of the story," says the owner. "No," says the tourist, "I was wondering if you have a bronze lawyer."

87   A lawyer and an engineer were fishing in the Caribbean. The lawyer said, "I'm here because my house burned down, and everything I owned was destroyed by the fire. The insurance company paid for everything." "That's quite a coincidence," said the engineer.

"I'm here because my house and all my belongings were destroyed by a flood, and my insurance company also paid for everything." The lawyer looked somewhat confused. "How do you start a flood?" he asked.

88   I tried to sue the airline for misplacing my luggage…I lost my case.

89   A snake and a rabbit were racing along a pair of intersecting forest pathways one day when they collided at the intersection. They immediately began to argue with one another as to who was at fault for the mishap. When the snake remarked that he had been blind since birth, and thus should be given additional leeway, the rabbit said that he, too, had been blind since birth. The two animals then forgot about the collision and began commiserating concerning the problems of being blind. The snake said that his greatest regret was the loss of his identity. He had never been able to see his reflection in the water, and for that reason did not know exactly what he looked like, or even what he was. The rabbit declared that he had the same problem. Seeing a way that they could help each other, the rabbit proposed that one feel the other from head to toe, and then try to describe what the other animal was. The snake agreed and started by winding himself around the rabbit. After a few moments, he announced, "You've got very soft, fuzzy fur, long ears, big rear feet, and a little fuzzy ball for a tail. I think that you must be a bunny rabbit!" The rabbit was much relieved to find his identity and proceeded to return the favor to the snake. After feeling about the snake's body for a few minutes, he asserted, "Well, you're scaly, you're slimy, you've got beady little eyes, you squirm and slither all the time, and you've got a forked tongue. I think you're a lawyer!"

90   A physician, an engineer, and an attorney were discussing who among them belonged to the oldest of the three professions represented. The physician said, "Remember, on the sixth day, God took a rib from Adam and fashioned Eve, making him the first surgeon. Therefore, medicine is the oldest profession." The engineer replied, "But before that, God created the heavens and earth from chaos and confusion, and thus He was the first engineer. Therefore, engineering is an older profession than medicine." Then, the lawyer spoke up. "Yes," he said, "But who do you think created all of the chaos and confusion?"

91   A young lawyer, starting up his private practice, was very anxious to impress potential clients. When he saw the first visitor to his office come through the door, he immediately picked up his phone and spoke into it. "I'm sorry, but my caseload is so tremendous that I'm not going to be able to look into your problem for at least a month. I'll have to get back to you then." He then turned to the man who had just walked in and said, "Now, what can I do for you?" "Nothing," replied the man. "I'm here to hook up your phone."

92   Lawyers are safe from the threat of automation taking over their professions. No one would build a robot to do nothing.

93   A doctor and a lawyer were attending a cocktail party when the doctor was approached by a man who asked advice on how to handle his ulcer. The doctor mumbled some medical advice, then turned to the lawyer and remarked, "I never know how to handle the situation when I'm asked for medical advice during a social function. Is it acceptable to send a bill for such advice?" The lawyer replied that it was certainly acceptable to do so. So, the next day, the doctor sent the ulcer-stricken man a bill. And the lawyer sent one to the doctor.

94   An engineer, a physicist, and a lawyer were being interviewed for a position as chief executive officer of a large corporation. The engineer was interviewed first and was asked a long list of questions, ending with "How much is two plus two?" The engineer excused himself and made a series of measurements and calculations before returning to the board room and announcing, "Four." The physicist was next interviewed and was asked the same questions. Again, the last question was, "How much is two plus two?" Before answering the last question, he excused himself, made for the library, and did a great deal of research. After a consultation with the United States Bureau of Standards and many calculations, he also announced, "Four." The lawyer was interviewed last, and again the final question was, "How much is two plus two?" The lawyer drew all the shades in the room, looked outside to see if anyone was there, checked the telephone for listening devices, and then whispered, "How much do you want it to be?"

95   As Mr. Smith was on his death bed, he attempted to formulate a plan that would allow him to take at least some of his considerable wealth with him. He called for the three men he trusted most—his lawyer, his doctor, and his clergyman. He told them, "I'm going to give you each $30,000 in cash before I die. At my funeral, I want you to place the money in my coffin so that I can try to take it with me." All three agreed to do this and were given the money. At the funeral, each approached the coffin in turn and placed an envelope inside. While riding in the limousine back from the cemetery, the clergyman said, "I have to confess something to you fellows. Brother Smith was a good churchman all his life, and I know he would have wanted me to do this. The church needed a new baptistery very badly, and I took $10,000 of the money he gave me and bought one. I only put $20,000 in the coffin." The physician then said, "Well, since we're confiding in one another, I might as well tell you that I didn't put the full $30,000 in the coffin either. Smith had a disease that could have been diagnosed sooner if I had this very new machine, but the machine cost $20,000 and I couldn't afford it then. I used $20,000 of the money to buy the machine so that I might be able to save another patient. I know that Smith would have wanted me to do that." The lawyer then said, "I'm ashamed of both of you. When I put my envelope into that coffin, it held my personal check for the full $30,000."

96   A lawyer charged a man $500 for legal services. The man paid him with crisp new $100 bills. After the client left, the lawyer discovered that two bills had stuck together...he'd been overpaid by $100. The ethical dilemma for the lawyer: should he tell his partner?

97   Did you hear about the new microwave lawyer? You spend eight minutes in his office and get billed as if you'd been there eight hours.

98   A Mexican bandit made a specialty of crossing the Rio Grande from time to time and robbing banks in Texas. Finally, a reward was offered for his capture, and an enterprising Texas ranger decided to track him down. After a lengthy search, he traced the bandit to his favorite cantina, snuck up behind him, put his trusty six-shooter to the bandit's head, and said, "You're under arrest. Tell me where you hid the loot, or I'll blow your brains out." But the bandit didn't speak English, and the Ranger didn't speak Spanish. Fortunately, a bilingual lawyer was in the saloon and translated the Ranger's message. The terrified bandit blurted out, in Spanish, that the loot was buried under the oak tree in back of the cantina. "What did he say?" asked the Ranger. The lawyer answered, "He said, 'Get lost, you turkey. You wouldn't dare shoot me.'"

99   A lawyer and his Czechoslovakian friend were camping in a backwoods section of Maine. Early one morning, the two went out to pick berries for their morning breakfast. As they went around the berry patch, gathering blueberries and raspberries in tremendous quantities, along came two huge bears—a male and a female. The lawyer, seeing the two bears, immediately dashed for cover. His friend, though, wasn't so lucky, and the male bear reached him and swallowed him whole. The lawyer ran back to his Mercedes, tore into town as fast as he could, and got the local backwoods sheriff. The sheriff grabbed his shotgun and dashed back to the berry patch with the lawyer. Sure enough, the two bears were still there. "He's in THAT one!" cried the lawyer, pointing to the male, while visions of lawsuits from his friend's family danced in his head. He just had to save his friend. The sheriff looked at the bears, and without batting an eye, levelled his gun, took careful aim, and shot the female. "Whatdidja do that for!" exclaimed the lawyer. "I said he was in the other!" "Exactly," replied the sheriff. "Would YOU believe a lawyer who told you the Czech was in the male?"

HEALTH
AND DOCTORS JOKES

100   Patient: Doctor, sometimes I feel like
I'm invisible.
Doctor: Who said that?

101   Patient: Doctor, I keep hearing a ringing sound.
Doctor: Then answer the phone!

102   Did you hear the one about the germ?
Never mind, I don't want to spread it around.

103   Hospital regulations require a wheelchair for
patients being discharged. However, while
working as a student nurse, I found one elderly
gentleman—already dressed and sitting on the
bed with a suitcase at his feet—who insisted he
didn't need my help to leave the hospital. After

a chat about rules being rules, he reluctantly let me wheel him to the elevator. On the way down, I asked him if his wife was meeting him. "I don't know," he said. "She's still upstairs in the bathroom changing out of her hospital gown."

104   The problem isn't that obesity runs in my family. The problem is that no one runs in my family.

105   My goal was to lose ten pounds this year. Only twenty to go!

106   There is only one way to look thin: hang out with fat people.

107   I do all the exercises every morning in front of the television: up, down, up, down, up, down. Then I do the other eyelid.

108   I can't believe I forgot to go to the gym today. That's seven years in a row now.

109   I'm so fat that the only way I can fit my whole body into a photo is to use panorama.

110 I've decided I need to quit my job as a personal trainer because I'm not big enough or strong enough. I've just handed in my too weak notice.

111 I was never a photogenic person because when everyone said cheese, I said, "WHERE?"

112 "Doctor, Doctor, will I be able to play the violin after the operation?"
"Yes, of course..."
"Great! I never could before!"

113 I got a job in a health club, but they said I wasn't fit for the job.

114 Refusing to go to the gym counts as resistance training, right?

115 I work out almost every day. Friday I almost worked out, Saturday I almost worked out, Sunday I almost worked out...

116 I'm in shape. Round is a shape.

117 Doctor: I have some bad news and some very bad news.
Patient: Well, might as well give me the bad news first.

Doctor: The lab called with your test results. They said you have twenty-four hours to live.
Patient: TWENTY-FOUR HOURS! That's terrible!! What could be worse? What's the bad news?
Doctor: I've been trying to reach you since yesterday.

118   Knock, knock! Who's there? Colin.
Colin who? Colin the doctor...I'm sick!

119   A man speaks frantically into the phone: "My wife is pregnant, and her contractions are only two minutes apart!"
"Is this her first child?" the doctor asks.
"No, you idiot!" the man shouts.
"This is her *husband*!"

120   A man walks into a doctor's office. He has a cucumber up his nose, a carrot in his left ear, and a banana in his right ear.
"What's the matter with me?" he asks the doctor.
The doctor replies, "You're not eating properly."

121   "The doctor said he would have me on my feet in two weeks."

"And did he?"
"Yes, I had to sell the car to pay the bill."

122   What did one tonsil say to the other tonsil?
Get dressed up—the doctor is taking us out!

123   Patient: I always see spots before my eyes.
Doctor: Didn't the new glasses help?
Patient: Sure, now I see the spots much
more clearly.

124   Doctor: Nurse, how is that little girl doing who
swallowed ten quarters last night?
Nurse: No change yet.

125   Patient: Doctor, I get heartburn every time I eat
birthday cake.
Doctor: Next time, take off the candles.

126   Does an apple a day keep the doctor away?
Only if you aim it well enough.

127   Why did the doctor tell the nurses to be quiet
when walking past the medicine cabinet? So
they wouldn't wake the sleeping pills!

128 What don't you want to hear in the middle of surgery?
"Where's my watch?"

129 Patient: Someone decided to graffiti my house last night!
Doctor: So why are you telling me?
Patient: I can't understand the writing.
Was it you?

130 The man told his doctor that he wasn't able to do all the things around the house that he used to do. When the examination was complete, he said: "Now, Doc, I can take it. Tell me in plain English what is wrong with me."
"Well, in plain English," the doctor replied, "you're just lazy."
"Okay," said the man. "Now give me the medical term so I can tell my wife."

131 "Doctor, there's a patient on Line 1 who says he's invisible."
"Well, tell him I can't see him right now."

132 Patient: Doctor, Doctor, I think I am losing my memory!
Doctor: When did that happen?
Patient: When did *what* happen?

133 Patient: Doctor, tell me how I can repay you for your kindness.
Doctor: You can pay by cash, check, or money order.

134 Why are doctors always calm? Because they have a lot of patients.

135 Why did the computer go to the doctor? She had a virus!

136 Patient: Doctor, Doctor, I'm going to die in fify-nine seconds!
Doctor: Hang on, I'll be there in a minute.

137 A skeleton went to the doctor. The doctor looked at the skeleton and said, "Aren't you a little late?"

138 Patient: Doctor, Doctor, I've got a strawberry stuck in my ear!
Doctor: Don't worry; I have some cream for that.

139 Why do surgeons wear masks? So no one will recognize them when they make a mistake.

140 The doctor stood by the bedside of a very sick patient and said, "I cannot hide the fact that you are very ill. Is there anyone you would like to see?"
"Yes," replied the patient faintly.
"Another doctor."

141 Why did the computer go to the doctor?
It thought it had a terminal illness.

142 How did the doctor cure the invisible man? He took him to the ICU.

143 Patient: Doctor, doctor, I'm addicted to brake fluid.
Doctor: Nonsense, man—you can stop anytime.

144 Why did the banana go to the doctor? He wasn't *peeling* well.

145 Two years ago, my doctor told me I was going deaf. I haven't heard from him since.

146 Patient: Doctor, Doctor, I feel like a dog.
Doctor: How long have you felt like this?
Patient: Since I was a puppy.

147 What do you get when a doctor goes back in time to teach himself medicine?
A pair o'docs.

148 I still remember the day the doctor told me I was mute...I had no words.

149 Patient: Doctor, you told me I have a month to live, and then you sent me a bill for $1,000. I can't pay that before the end of the month!
Doctor: Okay...you have six months to live.

150 The doctor took his patient into the room and said, "I have some good news and some bad news."
The patient said, "Give me the good news first."
"They're going to name the disease after you."

151 Receptionist: The doctor is so funny; he'll soon have you in stitches.
Patient: I hope not—I only came in for a checkup.

152 As I was admitted to the hospital for a procedure, the clerk asked for my wrist, saying, "I'm going to give you a bracelet."
"Has it got rubies and diamonds?" I asked coyly.
"No," he said. "But it costs just as much."

153   A man was wheeling himself frantically down the hall of the hospital in his wheelchair just before his operation.

A nurse stopped him and asked, "What's the matter?"

He said, "I heard the nurse say, 'It's a very simple operation; don't worry. I'm sure it will be all right.'"

"She was just trying to comfort you. What's so frightening about that?"

"She wasn't talking to me. She was talking to the doctor."

154   Who is the coolest doctor in the hospital? The hip consultant.

155   A hypochondriac told his doctor he was certain he had a fatal disease.

"Nonsense," scolded the doctor. "You wouldn't know if you had that. With that particular disease, there's no discomfort of any kind."

"Oh no!" gasped the patient. "Those are my symptoms exactly!"

156   How did you find that doctor was fake? He had good handwriting.

ANIMAL JOKES

157   What do you call a sleeping bull? A bull-dozer.

158   What do you get from a pampered cow? Spoiled milk.

159   What did the farmer call the cow that had no milk? An udder failure.

160   Why are teddy bears never hungry? They are always stuffed.

161   Why do fish live in salt water? Because pepper makes them sneeze.

162   What do you call lending money to a bison? A buff-a-loan.

163 What is the snake's favorite subject? Hiss-story.

164 How does a mouse feel after it takes a shower? Squeaky clean.

165 What is a cheetah's favorite food? Fast food.

166 What does a duck with hiccups lay? Scrambled eggs.

167 Why do ducks fly south for the winter? Because it's too far to walk.

168 What did the duck say to the waiter when the check came? Put it on my bill, please.

169 Why don't ducks grow up? Because they only grow down.

170 What is as big as an elephant but weighs nothing? Its shadow.

171 What do ducks put in their soup? Quackers.

172 What happens when you cross a wolf with a sheep? You have to get a new sheep.

173   Why did the duck cross the construction site?
To see a person lay a brick.

174   What does a frog eat with his hamburger?
French flies.

175   What do you call a sarcastic duck?
A wise quacker.

176   What dog keeps the best time? A watchdog.

177   Why did the duck cross the playground?
To get to the other slide.

178   Where do tough ducks come from?
Hard-boiled eggs.

179   Why did the Dalmatian go to the eye doctor?
He kept seeing spots.

180   What is the best way to catch a squirrel?
Act like a nut.

181   What did the judge say when the skunk walked
into the court room? Odor in the court.

182   Why did the snake cross the road?
To get to the other sssssside.

183   Why are fish so smart? Because they live
in schools.

184   Why is a fish easy to weigh? Because it has its
own scales.

185   What do you get when a chicken lays an egg on
top of a barn? An eggroll.

186   Why didn't the boy believe the tiger?
He thought it was a lion.

187   What happens when a frog's car breaks down?
He gets toad away.

188   What did one flea say to the other flea?
Shall we walk or take the dog?

189   What do you call an elephant in a phone
box? Stuck.

190   What do you call a baby bear with no teeth?
A gummy bear.

191 What do you call an angry monkey?
Furious George.

192 What is a cat's favorite color? Purr-ple.

193 What do ducks watch on TV? Duck-umentaries.

194 What's in the middle of a jellyfish?
It's jelly-button.

195 Why are cats bad storytellers?
Because they only have one tale.

196 A pony went to see the doctor because
it couldn't speak. "I know what's wrong,"
said the doctor. "You're a little horse!"

197 What's the most musical part of a chicken?
The drumstick!

198 What kind of ant is even bigger than an
elephant? A gi-ant!

199 What do you give a dog with a fever? Ketchup.
It's the best thing for a hot dog!

200   Where do you find a dog with no legs?
Where you left it.

201   What do you call a fish without an eye? Fsh!

202   How did the little Scottish dog feel when he saw
a monster? Terrier-fied!

203   Why are leopards no good at playing hide
and seek? Because they're always spotted.

204   Why do crabs never share?
Because they're shellfish.

205   Which kinds of snakes are found on cars?
Windshield vipers!

206   Why are elephants never rich?
Because they work for peanuts!

COMMUNIST JOKES

207 "Lenin has died, but his cause lives on!"
(An actual slogan.) Rabinovich notes: "I would
prefer it the other way around."

208 One old Communist says to another:
"No, my friend, we will not live long enough to
see communism succeed, but our children...our
poor children!"

209 How do you deal with mice in the Kremlin?
Put up a sign saying "Collective Farm." Then half
the mice will starve, and the rest will run away.

210 A new arrival to Gulag is asked: "What were you
given ten years for?"—"For nothing!"—"Don't
lie to us here, now! Everybody knows 'for
nothing' is three years."

211   "Is it hard to be in the Gulag?" —"Only for the first ten years."

212   What's the difference between a capitalist fairy tale and a Marxist fairy tale? A capitalist fairy tale begins, "Once upon a time, there was…" A Marxist fairy tale begins, "Someday, there will be…"

213   Is it true that there is freedom of speech in the USSR, just like in the USA? Yes. In the USA, you can stand in front of the White House in Washington, DC, and yell, "Down with the USA," and you will not be punished. Equally, you can also stand in Red Square in Moscow and yell, "Down with the USA," and you will not be punished.

214   What is the difference between the Constitutions of the US and USSR? Both of them guarantee freedom of speech. Yes, but the Constitution of the USA also guarantees freedom after the speech.

215   Is it true that the Soviet Union is the most progressive country in the world? Of course! Life was already better yesterday than it's going to be tomorrow!

216 Stalin attends the premiere of a Soviet comedy movie. He laughs and grins throughout the film, but after it ends, he says, "Well, I liked the comedy. But that clown had a moustache just like mine. Shoot him." Everyone is speechless, until someone sheepishly suggests, "Comrade Stalin, maybe the actor could shave off his moustache?" Stalin replies, "Good idea! First shave, then shoot!"

217 Child: When I grow up, I want to be a socialist.
Parent: You can't do both.

218 At a May Day parade, a very old Russian carries a placard that reads, "Thank you, comrade Stalin, for my happy childhood!" A party representative approaches the old man. "What's that? Are you mocking our party? Everyone can see that when you were a child, Comrade Stalin hadn't yet been born!" The old man replies, "That's precisely why I'm grateful to him!"

219 "I'm a socialist drinker!" The bartender chuckled and asked me, "Don't you mean social drinker?" "No, I only drink when someone else is paying."

220 An English athlete, a French athlete, and a Russian athlete are all on the medal podium at the 1976 Summer Olympics, chatting before the medal ceremony. "Don't get me wrong," says the Englishman, "winning a medal is very nice, but I still feel the greatest pleasure in life is getting home after a long day, putting one's feet up, and having a nice cup of tea." "You Englishman," snorts the Frenchman, "you have no sense of life. The greatest pleasure in life is sitting on the couch at home drinking a fine wine." "You are both wrong," scoffs the Russian. "The greatest pleasure in life is when you are sleeping at home and the KGB breaks your door down at 3 a.m., bursts into your room, and says, 'Ivan Ivanovitch, you are under arrest,' and you can reply, 'Sorry, comrade, Ivan Ivanovitch lives next door.'"

221 A man walks into a shop and asks, "You wouldn't happen to have any fish, would you?" The shop assistant replies, "You've got it wrong—ours is a butcher's shop. We don't have any meat. You're looking for the fish shop across the road. *There* they don't have any fish!"

222 How do you starve a socialist? You hide their food stamps under their work boots.

223 What happens if Soviet socialism comes to Saudi Arabia? First five years, nothing; then a shortage of sand.

224 Socialist jokes aren't funny. Unless everybody gets them.

225 How many socialists does it take to screw in a light bulb? Just one, but when it inevitably fails, they will be sure to inform us it wasn't a real light bulb.

226 "I want to sign up for the waiting list for a car. How long is it?" "Precisely ten years from today." "Morning or evening?" "Why, what difference does it make?" "The plumber's due in the morning."

227 It's the Soviet Union in the 1980s. A man has been standing in line at a butcher shop for seven hours when the butcher announces, "Comrades, I am sorry to inform you we are out of meat."
The man blows his top.
"I am a worker! I am a socialist! I am a veteran of the Great Patriotic War! And now you tell me that you're out of meat! This country stinks!"
A large man in a trench coat approaches.

"Comrade, comrade, calm yourself," he says. "You know what would have happened to you in the old days if you talked this way." The large man makes a thumb and forefinger motion at his temple. "So please, comrade, go home." The man goes home empty-handed, and his wife asks, "Are they out of meat?" "Worse than that," says the man. "They're out of bullets."

228   A farm worker greets Josef Stalin at his potato farm. "Comrade Stalin, we have so many potatoes that, piled one on top of the other, they would reach all the way to God," the farmer excitedly tells his leader. "But God does not exist," replies Stalin. "Exactly," says the farmer. "Neither do the potatoes."

229   "Granddaughter, please explain Communism to me," an old Russian woman asks her granddaughter. "How will people live under it? They probably teach you all about it in school." "Of course they do, Granny," her granddaughter responds. "When we reach Communism, the shops will be full—there'll be butter, and meat, and sausages...you'll be able to go and buy anything you want..." "Ah!" exclaimed the old woman joyfully. "Just like under the Tsar!"

230 What is very large, makes a lot of smoke and noise, takes down twenty liters of gas per hour, and cuts an apple into three pieces? The Soviet machine built to cut apples into four pieces.

231 What does a Soviet optimist say? It can't get any worse!

232 How do you know if someone is a socialist? Don't worry, they'll tell you.

233 Under communism, every man has what he needs. That's why the butcher puts a sign up that says, "Nobody needs meat today."

234 Two brothers, John and Bob, who lived in America and were members of the communist party, decided to emigrate to the USSR. Even though they didn't believe the American media's negative reports on the conditions in the USSR, they decided to exercise caution. John would go to Russia to test the waters. If they were right and it was a communist paradise, then John would write a letter to Bob using black ink. If, though, the situation in the USSR was as bad as the American media liked to portray, and the KGB was a force to be feared, John would use red ink to indicate whatever he says in the letter must not be believed. After three months John sent his first report. It was in black ink and read, "I'm so happy here! It's a beautiful country, and I enjoy complete freedom and a high standard of living. All the capitalist press wrote was lies. Everything is readily available! There is only one small thing of which there's a shortage. Red ink."

235   What did communists use to light their houses before candles? Electricity.

236   What is communism? The longest and most painful road to capitalism.

237   I once saw a group of communists. They were playing Soviet Roulette. It's like regular Russian Roulette, except that everyone dies equally.

238   What's the best way to kill communists? Communism.

239   Communist cars are unreliable. They're always Stalin.

240   Arkansas is the most communist state. Because it's not YOUR Kansas, it's OUR Kansas.

241 I just found out I've been dating a communist...I should have seen the red flags sooner.

242 Hello, welcome to today's communist marathon...On your Marx...

243 I'm beginning to suspect my cat is secretly a Chinese communist. All she ever talks about is Mao.

244 Communists shouldn't go to school. Don't they believe in a classless society?

245 A rich man visits Karl Marx as he's writing the Communist Manifesto. He asks: "So what's in that book of yours, Mr. Marx?" Marx replies: "None of your business."

246 Why do communists prefer to use only lowercase letters? Well, because they hate capitalism.

247 The chairman of the Communist Party decides to go check how his fellow comrades are doing. He walks into a dreadful cinema and sits down. Before the movie starts, there are fifteen minutes of communist propaganda, with him giving a boring speech at the end. Everyone stands up and starts clapping and cheering enthusiastically. The chairman is so humbled and stays seated, soaking in the love. A few minutes into the cheering, the guy on his left bends over and whispers directly in his ear. "Comrade, I know how you feel, but if don't want to be sent to Siberia, you better stand and clap."

248 Why do the cops pull over communists on their way to work? Because they are Russian.

249 Why do communists drink Herbal tea? Because proper tea is theft.

250 On second thought, maybe Communist America wouldn't be such a bad idea…We could all stand to lose a few pounds.

251 The regional KGB headquarters suffered a major fire and was almost completely destroyed. Shortly after, a man called looking for help. "I'm sorry, we can't do anything," said the receptionist. "The KGB has burnt down." Five minutes later, the receptionist received another call. "I'm sorry, we can't help. The KGB has burnt down." Another five minutes passed, and the phone rang again. The receptionist recognized the voice as the man who'd twice called previously. "Why do you keep calling? I told you that the KGB has burnt down." "I know. I just like hearing it."

252 A schoolboy wrote in his weekly essay: "My cat just had seven kittens. They're all communist." The following week, the boy wrote: "My cat's kittens are all capitalist." The teacher called him up and asked him to explain the sudden change. "Last week, you said they were all communists!" The boy nodded. "They were, but this week they all opened their eyes."

253 A worker standing in a liquor line says: "I have had enough, save my place, I am going to shoot Gorbachev." Two hours later he returns to claim his place in line. His friends ask, "Did you get him?" "No, the line there was even longer than the line here."

254 A regional Communist Party meeting is held to celebrate the anniversary of the Great October Socialist Revolution. The chairman gives a speech: "Dear comrades! Let's look at the amazing achievements of our Party after the revolution. For example, Maria here, who was she before the revolution? An illiterate peasant; she had but one dress and no shoes. And now? She is an exemplary milkmaid known throughout the entire region. Or look at Ivan Andreev. He was the poorest man in this village; he had no horse, no cow, not even an axe. And now? He is a tractor driver with two pairs of shoes! Or Trofim Semenovich Alekseev— he was a nasty hooligan, a drunk, and a dirty gadabout. Nobody would trust him with as much as a snowdrift in wintertime, as he would steal anything he could get his hands on. And now he's secretary of the Party Committee!"

255 In Russia we only had two TV channels: Channel One was propaganda, and Channel Two consisted of a KGB officer telling you, "Turn back at once to Channel One."

256 I asked my Russian friend how it was there; he said he couldn't complain.

WRITING JOKES

257   I invented a new word...Plagiarism!

258   What rhymes with orange? No, it doesn't.

259   When I first read the dictionary, I thought it was a long poem about everything.

260   Exaggerations have become an epidemic.
They went up by a million percent last year.

261   The world tongue-twister champion just got arrested. I hear they're gonna give him a really tough sentence.

262   I bought the world's worst thesaurus yesterday. Not only is it terrible, it's terrible.

263   You know what they say about cliffhangers.

264   A hyperbole is an exaggerated claim. No, really, reallllllllllyyyyy exaggerated. I mean, like, the most exaggerated thing in the history-of-ever!!

265   What do you call a place where everyone's a writer? A writer's block.

266   How many mystery novel writers does it take to change a lightbulb? Two. One to screw it in almost all the way, and another one to give it a surprising twist at the end.

267   Did you hear about the writer who became a baker? They say he makes excellent synonym rolls.

268   Why don't escaped convicts make good writers? Because they never finish their sentences.

269   There was once a young man who, in his youth, professed a desire to become a "great" writer. When asked to define "great," he said, "I want to write stuff that the whole world will read, stuff that people will react to on a truly emotional level, stuff that will make them scream, cry, and wail in desperation and anger!" He now works for Microsoft, writing error messages.

270 The writer Stephen King has a son named Joe...I'm not joking, but he is.

271 What's it like to be an aspiring writer? It's difficult to put into words.

272 The Prime Minister's speech writer has resigned. He's speechless.

273 I told my old classmate at our ten-year reunion that I'm a writer. "Oh yeah?" he asks. "Have you sold anything yet?" I said, "Sure. My house, my car, and all my stuff."

274 Being a writer is enjoyable. But the job of editor is more rewording.

275 Why do writers always feel cold? Because they are surrounded by drafts!

276 What's the motto of the American Writers Guild? YOU ESSAY! YOU ESSAY!

277   Did you hear about the writer that became a tailor? He had to make an Ernest living, the Hemingway.

278   My friend from Prague is a writer. He likes to use Spellczech.

279   What's the difference between a park bench and a writer? A park bench can support a family.

280   What do you get when you cross a writer with a deadline? A really clean house.

281   Three guys are sitting at a bar. First one says, "Yeah, I make $75,000 a year after taxes." Second one asks, "What do you do for a living?" "I'm a stockbroker," he replies, "and how much do you make?" "I should clear $60,000 this year." "What do you do?" "I'm an architect." The third guy has been sitting there quietly, staring into his beer, when the others turn to him. "Hey, how much do you make per year?" "I guess about $13,000." "Oh yeah? What kind of stories do you write?"

282   Let's eat kids. Let's eat, kids. Use a comma. Save lives.

283   I like cooking my family and my pets.
Use commas. Don't be a psycho.

284   Irony is when someone writes, "Your an idiot."
Use grammar. Insult properly.

285   I wrote a few children's books. Not on purpose.

286   A visitor to a certain college paused to admire the new Hemingway Hall that had been built on campus. "It's a pleasure to see a building named for Ernest Hemingway," he said. "Actually," said his guide, "it's named for Joshua Hemingway. No relation." The visitor was astonished. "Was Joshua Hemingway a writer, also?" "Yes, indeed," said his guide. "He wrote a check."

287   A linguistics professor was lecturing to his English class one day. "In English," he said, "a double negative forms a positive. In some languages, though, such as Russian, a double negative is still a negative. However, there is no language wherein a double positive can form a negative." A voice from the back of the room piped up, "Yeah, right."

288   Write a wise saying, and your name will live forever. – *Anonymous*.

289   Like, literally.

290   Today my best friend asked, "Can you lend me a book mark?" I immediately burst into tears. We've been close for years, and he doesn't know my name is Brian!

CORONA JOKES

291   Never in my life would I imagine that my hands would consume more alcohol than my mouth.

292   Nurse to patient: You've been in a coma since February—welcome back to the world! Patient: YAY! I can't wait to get out and join large social gatherings.

293   Has anyone told the Amish what is going on?

294   Unfortunately, since the quarantine, I can only tell inside jokes.

295   Sign at store: "We're out of toilet paper. Next shipment arriving 2050."

296   Why did the chicken cross the road? Because the chicken behind it didn't know how to socially distance properly.

297   Two grandmothers were bragging about their precious darlings. One of them says to the other, "Mine are so good at social distancing, they won't even call me."

298   Whose idea was it to sing "Happy Birthday" while washing your hands? Now every time I go to the bathroom, my kids expect me to walk out with a cake.

299   My husband purchased a world map and then gave me a dart and said, "Throw this and wherever it lands—that's where I'm taking you when this pandemic ends." Turns out, we're spending two weeks behind the fridge.

300   My mom always told me I wouldn't accomplish anything by lying in bed all day. But look at me now, Ma! I'm saving the world!

301   After years of wanting to thoroughly clean my house but lacking the time, this week I discovered that wasn't the reason.

302 If I keep stress-eating at this level, the buttons on my shirt will start socially distancing from each other.

303 Every few days, try your jeans on just to make sure they fit. Pajamas will have you believe all is well in the kingdom.

304 Yesterday I ran out of soap and body wash, and all I could find was dish detergent. Then it *Dawned* on me.

305 I never thought the comment "I wouldn't touch them with a six-foot pole" would become a national policy, but here we are!

306 I'm not talking to myself, I'm having a parent-teacher conference.

307 This morning I saw a neighbor talking to her cat. It was obvious she thought her cat understood her. I came into my house and told my dog. We laughed a lot.

308 Nothing like relaxing on the couch after a long day of being tense on the couch.

309   Knock, knock! Who is there? Seriously, don't touch my door and get back six meters to social distance.

310   Day 121 at home, and the dog is looking at me like, "See? This is why I chew the furniture!"

311   Why do they call it the novel coronavirus? It's a long story...

312   Why don't chefs find coronavirus jokes funny? They're in bad taste.

313   What should you do if you don't understand a coronavirus joke? Be patient.

314   I'll tell you a coronavirus joke now, but you'll have to wait two weeks to see if you get it.

315   Finland just closed its borders. You know what that means. No one will be crossing the finnish line.

316   Yeah, I have plans tonight. I'll probably hit the living room around eight or nine.

317   Why didn't the sick guy get the joke?
It flu over his head.

318   What did the sick parent make their kids
for lunch? Mac and sneeze.

319   It is fitting that coronavirus started in
Communist China because everyone is going
to get it.

MARRIAGE JOKES

320 I just asked my husband if he remembers what today is...scaring men is easy.

321 Have you ever noticed that a woman's "I'll be ready in five minutes" and a man's "I'll be home in five minutes" are exactly the same?

322 She wanted a puppy. But I didn't want a puppy. So, we compromised and got a puppy.

323 After finishing our Chinese food, my husband and I cracked open our fortune cookies.
Mine read, "Be quiet for a little while."
His read, "Talk while you have a chance."

324 I know of no one who is happily married except my husband.

325 Behind every angry woman is a man who has absolutely no idea what he did wrong.

326 Google request: How to disable autocorrect in wife.

327 I told my wife she was drawing her eyebrows too high. She looked surprised.

328 My wife screeched, "You haven't listened to one word I've said, have you!?" What a strange way to start a conversation with me.

329 A man got up one morning and couldn't find his alarm clock, so he asked his wife what had become of it. She said, "It went off at 6 o'clock."

330 A man is reading his newspaper and says to his wife: "Michelle, look. Here is an article about how women use about twice as many words per day as men do." The wife responds: "That's because we have to tell you everything twice."

331 My wife was complaining last night that I never listen to her. Or something like that...

332   Husband brings the child home from kindergarten and asks his wife, "He's been crying the whole way home. Is he sick or something?" "No," replies the wife, "he was just trying to tell you he isn't our Frankie."

333   A man and woman had been married for more than sixty years. They had shared everything. They had talked about everything. They had kept no secrets from each other, except that the little old woman had a shoe box in the top of her closet that she had cautioned her husband never to open or ask her about. For all of these years, he had never thought about the box, but one day, the little old woman got very sick, and the doctor said she would not recover. In trying to sort out their affairs, the little old man took down the shoe box and took it to his wife's bedside. She agreed that it was time that he should know what was in the box. When he opened it, he found two crocheted dolls and a stack of money totaling $95,000. He asked her about the contents. "When we were to be married," she said, "my grandmother told me the secret of a happy marriage was to never argue. She told me that if I ever got angry with you, I should just keep quiet and crochet a doll." The little old man was so moved; he had to fight back tears. Only two precious dolls were in the box. She had only been angry with him two times in all those years of living and loving. He almost burst with happiness. "Honey," he said, "that explains the dolls, but what about all of this money? Where did it come from?" "Oh," she said. "That's the money I made from selling the dolls."

334 A wife was making a breakfast of fried eggs for her husband. Suddenly, her husband burst into the kitchen. "Careful," he said, "CAREFUL! Put in some more butter! Oh my gosh! You're cooking too many at once. TOO MANY! Turn them! TURN THEM NOW! We need more butter. Oh my gosh! WHERE are we going to get MORE BUTTER? They're going to STICK! Careful. CAREFUL! I said be CAREFUL! You NEVER listen to me when you're cooking! Never! Turn them! Hurry up! Are you CRAZY? Have you LOST your mind? Don't forget to salt them. You know you always forget to salt them. Use the salt. USE THE SALT! THE SALT!" The wife stared at him. "What in the world is wrong with you? You think I don't know how to fry a couple of eggs?" The husband calmly replied, "I just wanted to show you what it feels like when I'm driving."

335 "Mom, Dad, sit down. I have something very important to tell you," said Samantha, upon her return home from college after graduation. "I met a guy who lives near the college that I really like, and we decided we are going to get married!" "Oh Samantha! I am so happy for you!" gushed her mom, giving her a big hug. "I hope you two will be really happy together! I can't wait to meet him!" "Tell us more about him," said her dad, "does he have any money?" "Oh Dad! Is that all you men ever think about? That was the first question he asked me about you too!"

336   Men: Once you get married, remember that when you have a discussion with your wife, always get the last two words in: "Yes, dear."

337   My wife gave birth four times and still fits into her prom dress from high school. I gave birth zero times and I haven't fit into my pants since March.

338   At every party there are two kinds of people: those who want to go home and those who don't. The trouble is, they are usually married to each other.

339   The only one of your children who does not grow up and move away is your husband.

340 I always wanted to marry Mrs. Right, but I didn't know her first name was "Always."

341 My wife keeps telling everyone that she can read their minds, but she never can. She's tele-pathetic.

342 The husband is a very talented man. Very talented indeed...He's a gifted inventor, a shrewd businessman, a deep thinker, and a noted connoisseur of the arts. He's so talented he can fake all of that.

343 Outvoted 1-1 by my wife again.

344 Man is incomplete until he is married. Then he is really finished.

345 The best way to get most husbands to do something is to suggest that perhaps they're too old to do it.

346 Marriage is the alliance of two people, one of whom never remembers birthdays and the other who never forgets them.

347   Wife: Do you want dinner? Husband: Sure, what are my choices? Wife: Yes and no.

348   Marriages are made in heaven. Then again, so are thunder, lightning, tornadoes, and hail.

349   My wife and I always compromise. I admit I'm wrong, and she agrees with me.

350   When your spouse gets a little upset, just remember a simple "calm down" in a soothing voice is all it takes to get them to be a lot more upset.

351   Every time you talk to your wife, your mind should remember: "This conversation will be recorded for training and quality purposes."

352   There was a woman who said, "I never knew what real happiness was until I got married, and then it was too late."

353   Did you hear about the two cellphones that got married? The reception was perfect.

354 Marriage lets you annoy one special person for the rest of your life. Take advantage of that as much as you can.

355 Every married man should forget his mistakes. There's no use in two people remembering the same thing.

356 I asked my wife what she wanted for a birthday present. She told me, "Nothing would make me happier than a diamond necklace." So I bought her nothing.

357 I think men who have a pierced ear are better prepared for marriage. They've experienced pain and bought jewelry.

358 "By all means, marry; if you get a good wife/ husband, you'll be happy. If you get a bad one, you'll become a philosopher."—Socrates

359 Only after getting married do you realize that those husband-wife jokes were not just jokes.

360 They married for better or for worse. He couldn't have done better, and she couldn't have done worse!

361   There are two times when a man doesn't understand a woman: before marriage and after marriage.

362   After two years of happy marriage, the bride confessed one day that she had just bought twelve new dresses. "Twelve!" exclaimed the groom. "What could anyone want with twelve new dresses?" She replied, "Twelve new pairs of shoes, of course."

363   I had my credit card stolen the other day, but I didn't bother to report it because the thief spends less than my wife.

364   I once gave my husband the silent treatment for an entire week, at the end of which he declared, "Hey, we're getting along pretty well lately!"

365   The length of a marriage is inversely proportional to the amount of money spent on the wedding.

366   The secret to having your husband come home from work on time? Tell him dinner starts at 6 p.m. sharp—whether he's there or not.

367 There are only two rules for a happy marriage: 1) Your wife is always right. 2) When you think you're right, remind yourself of rule #1.

368 A wise man once said, "I don't know...ask my wife."

369 My wife says I'm too competitive. I told her I already knew that.

370 The one who snores will fall asleep first.

KNOCK-KNOCK JOKES

371 Knock, knock! Who's there? Theodore!
Theodore who? Theodore wasn't open,
so I knocked.

372 Knock, knock! Who's there? Amos.
Amos who? A mosquito.

373 Knock, knock! Who's there? Canoe!
Canoe who? Canoe come out and play
with me today?

374 Knock, knock! Who's there? Canoe.
Canoe who? Canoe open the door?

375 Knock, knock! Who's there? Who!
Who, who? That's what an owl says!

376 Knock, knock! Who's there? Lettuce.
Lettuce who? Lettuce in, it's cold out here.

377 Knock, knock! Who's there? Honeybee.
Honeybee who? Honeybee a dear and get me
some juice.

378 Knock, knock! Who's there? Wooden shoe.
Wooden shoe who? Wooden shoe like to hear
another joke?

379 Knock, knock! Who's there? A broken pencil.
A broken pencil who? Oh, never mind, it's
pointless.

380 Knock, knock! Who's there? Cow says.
Cow says who? No silly, a cow says Mooooo!

381 Knock, knock! Who's there? Mikey!
Mikey who? Mikey doesn't fit in the keyhole.

382 Knock, knock! Who's there? Atch.
Atch who? Bless you!

383 Knock, knock! Who's there? I am.
I am who? You don't know who you are?

384   Knock, knock! Who's there? Ya.
Ya who? Wow, I'm excited to see you too.

385   Knock, knock! Who's there? Figs.
Figs who? Figs the doorbell, it's broken!

386   Knock, knock! Who's there? Boo!
Boo who? Don't cry, it's just me.

387   Knock, knock! Who's there? Interrupting pirate!
Interrup... ARRRRRRRRRR!

388   Knock, knock! Who's there? Iva.
Iva who? I've a sore hand from knocking!

389   Knock, knock! Who's there? A little old lady.
A little old lady who? I didn't know you
could yodel.

390   Will you remember me in two minutes? Yes.
Knock, knock! Who's there? Hey, you didn't
remember me!

391   Knock, knock! Who's there? Banana.
Banana who? Knock, knock! Who's there?
Banana. Banana who? Knock, knock! Who's
there? Banana. Banana who? Knock, knock!

Who's there? Orange. Orange who? Orange you glad I didn't say banana?

392 Knock, knock! Who's there? Howard!
Howard who? Howard I know?

393 Knock, knock! Who's there? Beets!
Beets who? Beets me!

394 Knock, knock! Who's there? Ice cream!
Ice cream who? Ice cream if you don't let me in!

395 Knock, knock, Who's there? Cows!
Cows who? Cows go "moo" not who!

396 Knock, knock! Who's there? Tank!
Tank who? You're welcome!

397 Knock, knock! Who's there? Luke!
Luke who? Luke through the keyhole and you can see.

398 Knock, knock! Who's there? Frank!
Frank who? Frank you for being my friend!

399 Knock, Knock! Who's there? Will.
Will who? Will you let me in? It's freezing out here!

400   Knock, knock! Who's there? Olive.
Olive who? Olive right next door to you.

401   Knock, knock! Who's there? Turnip.
Turnip who? Turnip the volume,
it's quiet in here.

402   Knock, knock! Who's there? Orange.
Orange who? Orange you glad to see me?

403   Knock, knock! Who's there? Police.
Police who? Pa-lease may I come in?

404   Knock, knock! Who's there? Water.
Water who? Water you doing in my house?

405   Knock, knock! Who's there? Goat.
Goat who? Goat to the door and find out.

406   Knock, knock! Who's there? Beef.
Beef who? Before I get cold, you'd better
let me in!

407   Knock, knock! Who's there? Leaf.
Leaf who? Leaf me alone!

408 Knock, knock! Who's there? Nobel.
Nobel who? No bell, that's why I knocked!

409 Knock, knock! Who's there? Anita.
Anita who? Anita borrow a pencil!

410 Knock, knock! Who's there? Yukon.
Yukon who? Yukon say that again!

411 Knock, knock! Who's there? Amarillo.
Amarillo who? Amarillo nice guy!

412 Knock, knock! Who's there? Tyrone.
Tyrone who? Tyrone shoelaces!

413 Knock, knock! Who's there? Abie.
Abie who? Abie C D E F G H...

414 Knock, knock! Who's there? Amy.
Amy who? Amy fraid I've forgotten!

415 Knock, knock! Who's there? Cash.
Cash who? No thanks, but I'd like some peanuts.

416 Knock, knock! Who's there? Alpaca.
Alpaca who? Alpaca the trunk, you pack
the suitcase!

417   Knock, knock! Who's there? Alma.
          Alma who? Alma not going to tell you!

418   Knock, knock! Who's there? Ken.
          Ken who? Ken I come in, it's freezing out here?

419   Knock, knock! Who's there? Control freak.
          Con—Okay, now you say, "Control freak who?"

420   Knock, knock! Who's there? Impatient cow.
          Impatient co...MOO!

421   Knock, knock! Who's there? Wanda.
          Wanda who? Wanda hang out with me
          right now?

422   Knock, knock! Who's there? Snow.
          Snow who? Snow use. I forgot my name again!

423   Knock, knock! Who's there? Carmen.
          Carmen who? Carmen let me in already!

424   Knock, knock! Who's there? Sherlock.
          Sherlock who? Sherlock your door is shut tight.

425   Knock, knock! Who's there? Scold.
          Scold who? Scold outside—let me in!

426   Knock, knock! Who's there? Robin.
Robin who? Robin you! Hand over your cash!

427   Knock, knock! Who's there? Otto.
Otto who? Otto know what's taking
you so long!

428   Knock, knock! Who's there? Noah.
Noah who? Noah any place I can get a
bite to eat?

429   Knock, knock! Who's there? Needle.
Needle who? Needle little help gettin'
in the door.

430   Knock, knock! Who's there? Nana.
Nana who? Nana your business who's there.

431   Knock, knock! Who's there? Justin.
Justin who? Justin the neighborhood
and thought I'd come over.

432   Knock, knock! Who's there? Isabelle.
Isabelle who? Isabelle working, or should
I keep knocking?

433   Knock, knock! Who's there? Harry.
Harry who? Harry up and let me in!

434   Knock, knock! Who's there? Dozen.
Dozen who? Dozen anyone want to let me in?

435   Knock Knock! Who's there? Dishes.
Dishes who? Dishes me, who are you?

436   Knock, knock! Who's there? Dishes.
Dishes who? Dishes a nice place you got here.

437   Knock, knock! Who's there? Claire.
Claire who? Claire the way; I'm coming in!

438   Knock, knock! Who's there? Ben.
Ben who? Ben knocking for twenty minutes!

439   Knock, knock! Who's there? Howl.
Howl who? Howl you know it's really me unless
you open the door?

440   Knock, knock! Who's there? Wendy.
Wendy who? Wendy bell works again, I won't
have to knock anymore.

441 Knock, knock! Who's there? Alex.
Alex who? Hey, Alex the questions around here!

442 Knock, knock! Who's there? Alex.
Alex who? Alex-plain later!

443 Knock, knock! Who's there? Annie.
Annie who? Annie body going to open the
door already?

444 Knock, knock! Who's there? Somebody who
can't reach the doorbell!

445 Knock, knock! Who's there? Doris.
Doris who? Doris locked. Open up!

446 Knock, knock! Who's there? Goliath.
Goliath who? Goliath down, you look-eth tired!

447 Knock, knock! Who's there? From.
From who? Actually, grammatically speaking,
you should say "from whom."

448 Knock, knock! Who's there? Radio.
Radio who? Radio not, here I come!

449   Knock, knock! Who's there? Witches. Witches who? Witches the way home?

450   Knock, knock! Who's there? Doughnut! Doughnut who? Doughnut ask, it's a secret.

451   Knock, knock! Who's there? Justin! Justin who? Justin time for lunch.

452   Knock, knock! Who's there? Broccoli. Broccoli who? Broccoli doesn't have a last name, silly.

453   Knock, knock! Who's there? Cook! Cook who? Don't call me cuckoo!

454   Knock, knock! Who's there? Abby! Abby who? Abby birthday to you.

455   Knock, knock! Who's there? Water? Water who? Water way to answer the door!

456   Knock, knock! Who's there? Cargo! Cargo who? Car go "Beep beep!"

457   Knock, knock! Who's there? Ketchup. Ketchup who? Ketchup with me and I'll tell you!

458 Knock, knock! Who's there? Annie.
Annie who? Annie body home?

459 Knock, knock! Who's there? Watson.
Watson who? What's on the agenda tonight?

460 Knock, knock! Who's there? Spell.
Spell who? W-H-O.

461 Knock, knock! Who's there? Althea.
Althea who? Althea later alligator!

462 Knock, knock! Who's there? Norma Lee.
Norma Lee who? Norma Lee I don't go around
knocking on doors, but I just had to meet you!

463 Knock, knock! Who's there? CD.
CD who? CD guy on your doorstep?

464 Knock, knock! Who's there? Candice.
Candice who? Candice door open, or am
I stuck out here?

465 Knock, knock! Who's there? Iowa.
Iowa who? Iowa big apology to the owner
of that red car!

466 Knock, knock! Who's there? Abbot.
Abbot who? Abbot you don't know who this is!

467 Knock, knock! Who's there? Viper.
Viper who? Viper nose, it's running!

468 Knock, knock! Who's there? Anee.
Anee who? Anee one you like!

469 Knock, knock. Who's there? Stopwatch.
Stopwatch who? Stopwatch you're doing
and let me in!

470 Knock, knock! Who's there? Needle.
Needle who? Needle little money for
the movies.

471 Knock, knock! Who's there? Henrietta.
Henrietta who? Henrietta worm that was in
his apple!

472 Knock, knock! Who's there? Avenue.
Avenue who? Avenue knocked on this
door before?

473 Knock, knock! Who's there? Harry.
Harry who? Harry up, it's cold out here!

474   Knock, knock! Who's there? A herd.
A herd who? A herd you were home,
so I came over.

475   Knock, knock! Who's there? Adore.
Adore who? Adore is between us. Open up!

476   Knock, knock! Who's there? Otto.
Otto who? Otto know. I've got amnesia.

477   Knock, knock! Who's there? Amish.
Amish who? Really? You don't look like a shoe!

478   Knock, knock! Who's there? Max.
Max who? Max no difference to you,
just let me in!

479   Knock, Knock! Who's there? Annie.
Annie who? Annie thing you can do,
I can do better.

480   Knock, knock! Who's there? Ashe.
Ashe who? Bless you!

481   Knock, Knock! Who's there? Hike.
Hike who? I didn't know you liked
Japanese poetry!

482   Knock, knock! Who's there? Lettuce.
Lettuce who? Lettuce in and you'll find out!

483   Knock-knock! Who's there? Aaron.
Aaron who? Why Aaron you opening the door?

484   Knock, knock! Who's there? Hawaii.
Hawaii who? I'm fine, Hawaii you?

485   Knock, knock. Who's there? Gladys.
Gladys, who? Gladys the
weekend—no homework!

RIDDLES

486   What two things can you never eat
for breakfast? Lunch and dinner.

487   If you have it, you want to share it. If you share
it, you don't have it. What is it? A secret.

488   Why do mummy kangaroos always hate wet
days? Because their kids play inside.

489   What stays in its bed most of the day and
sometimes goes to the bank? A stream.

490   What has to be broken before it can be
used? An egg.

491   What did the baby corn say to its mom?
Where is the popcorn?

492   What kind of nuts always seems to have a cold? Cashews!

493   Waiter, will my pizza be long?
No sir, it will be round!

494   Why don't you starve in a desert?
Because of all the "sand which is" there.

495   How do you make a walnut laugh? Crack it up!

496   What do you give to a sick lemon? Lemon aid!

497   What kind of keys do kids like to carry? Cookies!

498   How can you tell that the ocean
is friendly? It waves.

499   What falls but never hits the ground?
The temperature!

500   Whom does everyone listen to,
but no one believes?
The weatherman.

501   Why did the leaf go to the doctor?
It was feeling green!

502 What kind of tree can fit into your hand?
A palm tree!

503 What did the tree do when the bank closed?
It started a new branch.

504 I'm named after nothing, though I'm awfully clamorous. And when I'm not working, your house is less glamorous. What am I?
A vacuum cleaner.

505 What can't be put in a saucepan? Its lid.

506 It belongs to you, but other people use it more than you do. What is it? Your name.

507 I'm tall when I'm young, and I'm short when I'm old. What am I? A candle.

508 What is cut on a table but is never eaten?
A deck of cards.

509 What month of the year has 28 days?
All of them.

510 What is full of holes but still holds water? A sponge.

511 What question can you never answer yes to? Are you asleep yet?

512 When is a well-dressed lion like a weed? When he's a dandelion (dandy lion).

513 How does a lion greet the other animals in the field? Pleased to eat you.

514 What happened when the lion ate the comedian? He felt funny!

515 What fish only swims at night? A starfish.

516 What is always in front of you but can't be seen? The future.

517 There's a one-story house in which everything is yellow. Yellow walls, yellow doors, yellow furniture. What color are the stairs? There aren't any—it's a one-story house.

518 What can you break, even if you never pick it up or touch it? A promise.

519 Why did the turkey cross the road? To prove he wasn't chicken!

520   What animals are on legal documents? Seals!

521   What do you get when you cross a snake
and a pie? A pie-thon!

522   What animal is "out of bounds?
An exhausted kangaroo!

523   What did the buffalo say to his son when he
went away on a trip? Bi-son!

524   What kind of coat is best put on wet?
A coat of paint.

525   How do bees get to school? By school buzz!

526   What do you call bears with no ears? B!

527   What animal has more lives than a cat?
Frogs, they croak every night!

528   What time is it when an elephant sits on the
fence? Time to fix the fence!

529   Why did the elephant sit on the marshmallow?
So he wouldn't fall into the hot chocolate.

530   Why are elephants so wrinkled? Did you ever try to iron one?

531   What do you do when you see an elephant with a basketball? Get out of its way!

532   What's the best thing to do if an elephant sneezes? Get out of its way!

533   What is gray and blue and very big?
An elephant holding its breath!

534   What time is it when ten elephants are chasing you? Ten after one!

535   How do you keep an elephant from charging?
You take away its credit cards!

536   What do you do with a blue elephant?
You try and cheer her up.

537   When does a teacher carry birdseed?
When there is a parrot-teacher conference.

538   What is a polygon? A dead parrot.

539 What kind of bird works at a construction site?
The crane!

540 Why do birds fly south in the winter?
Because it's too far to walk!

541 What did the sick chicken say?
Oh no! I have the people-pox!

542 What do you call a funny chicken?
A comedi-hen!

543 Why do scientists think hummingbirds hum?
Because they can't remember the words!

544 What bird is always depressed? The blue jay.

545 Why do seagulls like to live by the sea? Because
if they lived by the bay, they would be bagels!

546 A man who was outside in the rain without
an umbrella or hat didn't get a single hair
on his head wet. How? He was bald.

547 What's worse than raining cats and dogs?
"Hailing" taxi cabs!

548   What can you keep after giving it to someone?
Your word.

549   What game did the cat like to play with
the mouse? Catch.

550   Where did the school kittens go for their field
trip? To the mewseum.

551   Why did the cat go to medical school?
To become a first aid kit.

552   Who was the first cat to fly in an airplane?
Kitty-hawk.

553   Have you ever seen a catfish? No.
How could he hold the rod and reel?

554   Why did the poor dog chase his own tail?
He was trying to make both ends meet!

555   I shave every day, but my beard stays the same.
What am I? A barber.

556   Why don't dogs make good dancers?
Because they have two left feet!

557 What happens when it rains cats and dogs?
You can step in a poodle!

558 What did the dog say when he sat on sandpaper? Ruff!

559 What do you call a dog that is left-handed?
A southpaw!

560 You see a boat filled with people, yet there isn't a single person on board. How is that possible?
All the people on the boat are married.

561 What type of markets do dogs avoid?
Flea markets!

562 What did the cowboy say when his dog ran away? Well, doggone!

563 What time does a duck wake up?
At the quack of dawn!

564 What do ducks get after they eat? A bill!

565 What do you call a crate full of ducks?
A box of quackers!

566   Who stole the soap? The robber ducky!

567   What do you get if you cross fireworks with a duck? A firequacker!

568   What was the goal of the detective duck? To quack the case.

569   Why was the duck put into the basketball game? To make a fowl shot!

570   What did the duck do after he read all these jokes? He quacked up!

571   A man rode his horse to town on Monday. The next day, he rode back on Monday. How is this possible? The horse's name was Monday.

572   Why did the pony have to gargle? Because it was a little horse!

573   What did the horse say when it fell? I've fallen and I can't giddy-up.

574   What did the teacher say when the horse walked into the class? Why the long face?

575   What do you call a horse that lives next door?
A neigh-bor!

576   What's the best way to lead a horse to water?
With lots of apples and carrots!

577   What disease was the horse scared of getting?
Hay fever!

578   How long should a horse's legs be?
Long enough to reach the ground.

579   Which side of the horse has the most hair?
The outside!

580   Why did the man stand behind the horse?
He was hoping to get a kick out of it.

581   How do rabbits travel? By hare-plane.

582   What is a bunny's motto?
Don't be mad, be hoppy!

583   How do you catch a unique rabbit?
Unique up on it.

584 How do you know carrots are good for your eyes? Because you never see rabbits wearing glasses!

585 How did the farmer mend his pants? With cabbage patches!

586 What do you call a happy cowboy? A jolly rancher!

587 What has one head, one foot, and four legs? A bed.

588 Did you hear the joke about the roof? Never mind, it's over your head!

589 How many letters are in the alphabet? There are eleven letters in "the alphabet."

590 How can you spell cold with two letters? IC (icy).

591 David's father had three sons: Jon, Robert, and David!

592 If you were in a race and passed the person in second place, what place would you be in? Second place!

593   What is the center of gravity? The letter v!

594   What English word has three consecutive double letters? Bookkeeper.

595   What has a head, a tail, is brown, and has no legs? A penny!

596   The turtle took two chocolates to Texas to teach Thomas to tie his boots. How many t's are in that? There are two t's in THAT!

597   What gets bigger and bigger as you take more away from it? A hole!

598   I am an odd number. Take away a letter, and I become even. What number am I? Seven.

599   Can you spell rotted with two letters? DK (decay).

600   How many books can you put into an empty backpack? One! After that it's not empty.

601   Which weighs more, a ton of feathers or a ton of bricks? Neither, they both weigh a ton!

602   Does your shirt have holes in it? No.
Then how did you put it on?

603   What starts with a P and ends with an E
and has a million letters in it? A post office!

604   When does a cart come before a horse?
In the dictionary!

605   Mary has four daughters, and each of her
daughters has a brother. How many children
does Mary have? Five; each daughter has the
same brother.

606   What has two hands, a round face, always runs,
but stays in place? A clock!

607   What breaks when you say it? Silence!

608   How many peas are there in a pint?
There is one P in a 'pint.'

609   What did the ground say to the earthquake?
You crack me up!

610   Why did the music teacher need a ladder?
To reach the high notes.

611   How do you get straight A's? By using a ruler!

612   What object is king of the classroom? The ruler!

613   When do astronauts eat? At launch time!

614   What did the pen say to the pencil?
So, what's your point?

615   What did the pencil sharpener say to the pencil?
Stop going in circles and get to the point!

616   How does the barber cut the moon's hair?
E-clipse it!

617   What happened when the wheel was invented?
It caused a revolution!

618   What do librarians take with them when they
go fishing? Bookworms.

619   What is the world's tallest building?
The library, because it has the most stories.

620   What vegetables do librarians like? Quiet peas.

621   Why did the clock in the cafeteria run slow?
It always went back four seconds.

622   What has five eyes and a lot of water?
The Mississippi River.

623   What is the smartest state? Alabama, it has four
A's and one B.

624   What stays in the corner but travels around the
world? A stamp!

625   Where do pencils come from? Pennsylvania!

626   What is the capital of Washington? The W!

627   Why were the early days of history called the
dark ages? Because there were so many knights!

628   Why is England the wettest country?
Because the queen has reigned there for years!

629   How did the Vikings send secret messages?
By Norse code.

630   Who invented fractions? Henry the 1/4th.

631 What kind of lighting did Noah use for the ark? Floodlights.

632 What's purple and five thousand miles long? The grape wall of China.

633 Why aren't you doing well in history? Because the teacher keeps on asking about things that happened before I was born!

634 Where was the Declaration of Independence signed? At the bottom.

635 What is the fruitiest subject at school? History, because it's full of dates!

636 Why didn't the quarter roll down the hill with the nickel? Because it had more cents.

637 Why was the math book sad? Because it had too many problems.

638 What kind of meals do math teachers eat? Square meals!

639 Why didn't the two 4's want any dinner? Because they already 8!

640 What is a butterfly's favorite subject at school?
Mothematics.

641 What did zero say to the number eight?
Nice belt.

642 Teacher: Why are you doing your multiplication
on the floor? Student: You told me not to
use tables.

643 Why did the teacher wear sunglasses?
Because his class was so bright!

644 Why were the teacher's eyes crossed?
She couldn't control her pupils!

645 Why did the policeman go to the baseball
game? He heard someone had stolen a base!

646 Why did the book join the police? He wanted
to go undercover!

647 You walk into a room that contains a match,
a kerosene lamp, a candle, and a fireplace. What
would you light first? The match.

648 What do you call a flying police officer?
A heli-copper!

649 Why did the lazy man want a job in a bakery?
So he could loaf around!

650 Why did the farmer ride his horse to town?
It was too heavy to carry!

651 A man dies of old age on his 25th birthday.
How is this possible? He was born on
February 29.

652 The day before yesterday, I was 21,
and next year I will be 24. When is my birthday?
December 31; today is January 1.

653 What did one tooth say to the other tooth?
Thar's gold in them fills!

654 What did the judge say to the dentist?
Do you swear to pull the tooth, the whole
tooth, and nothing but the tooth?

655 Why did the tree go to the dentist?
To get a root canal.

656   Why did the king go to the dentist?
To get his teeth crowned!

657   What time do you go to the dentist?
Tooth-Hurty!

658   What does a dentist do during an earthquake?
He braces himself!

659   What did the tooth say to the dentist as he was leaving? Fill me in when you get back.

660   Has your tooth stopped hurting yet?
I don't know—the dentist kept it.

661   What did the dentist get for an award?
A little plaque.

662   When does a doctor get mad?
When he runs out of patients!

663   Why did the pillow go to the doctor?
He was feeling all stuffed up!

664   Where does a boat go when it's sick?
To the doc(k)!

ONE-LINERS

665   I hate people who use big words just to make themselves look perspicacious.

666   How did I escape Iraq? Iran.

667   Moses had the first tablet that could connect to the cloud.

668   I wasn't originally going to get a brain transplant, but then I changed my mind.

669   The first computer dates back to Adam and Eve. It was an Apple with limited memory, just one byte. And then everything crashed.

670   Today a man knocked on my door and asked for a small donation toward the local swimming pool. I gave him a glass of water.

671   I'm reading a book about anti-gravity. It's impossible to put down.

672   I changed my password to "incorrect." So whenever I forget what it is, the computer will say: "Your password is incorrect."

673   I find it ironic that the colors red, white, and blue stand for freedom until they are flashing behind you.

674   Just read that 4,153,237 people got married last year. Not to cause any trouble, but shouldn't that be an even number?

675   A recent study has found that women who carry a little extra weight live longer than the men who mention it.

676   I'm great at multitasking. I can waste time, be unproductive, and procrastinate all at once.

677 EBay is so useless. I tried to look up lighters, and all they had was 13,749 matches.

678 At what age is it appropriate to tell my dog that he's adopted?

679 According to most studies, people's number one fear is public speaking. Number two is death. Does that sound right? This means that for the average person attending a funeral, you're better off in the casket than doing the eulogy.

680 I'd tell you a chemistry joke, but I know I wouldn't get a reaction.

681 I used to think I was indecisive, but now I'm not too sure.

682 Feeling pretty proud of myself. The Sesame Street puzzle I bought said three to five years, but I finished it in eighteen months.

683 If you're not supposed to eat at night, why is there a light bulb in the refrigerator?

684 Don't trust atoms; they make up everything.

685 Did you know that dolphins are so smart that within a few weeks of captivity, they can train people to stand on the very edge of the pool and throw them fish?

686 I saw an ad for burial plots and thought to myself: this is the last thing I need.

687 I was addicted to the hokeypokey...
but thankfully, I turned myself around.

688 Just burned two thousand calories. That's the last time I leave brownies in the oven while I nap.

689 Women spend more time wondering what men are thinking than men spend thinking.

690 Apparently, I snore so loudly that it scares everyone in the car I'm driving.

691 A cop just knocked on my door and told me that my dogs were chasing people on bikes. My dogs don't even own bikes...

692 Never laugh at your wife's choices...
you're one of them.

693 I bought a vacuum cleaner six months ago, and so far all it's been doing is gathering dust.

694 I have a few jokes about unemployed people, but it doesn't matter—none of them work.

695 I entered what I ate today into my new fitness app, and it just sent an ambulance to my house.

696 To the mathematicians who thought of the idea of zero, thanks for nothing!

697 A computer once beat me at chess, but it was no match for me at kick boxing.

698 I like having conversations with kids. Grownups never ask me what my third favorite reptile is.

699 That awkward moment when you leave a store without buying anything, and all you can think is "Act natural, you're innocent."

700 People used to laugh at me when I would say, "I want to be a comedian." Well, nobody's laughing now.

701 Don't you hate it when someone answers their own questions? I do.

702 My mom said that if I don't get off my computer and do my homework, she'll slam my head on the keyboard—but I think she's jokinfjreoiwjrtwe4to8rkljreun8f4ny84c8y4t58ly m4wthylmhawt4mylt4amlathnatyn.

703 My wife is so negative. I remembered the car seat, the stroller, AND the diaper bag. Yet all she can talk about is how I forgot the baby.

704 Did you hear about the kidnapping at school? It's okay. He woke up.

705 Thanks for explaining the word "many" to me, it means a lot.

706 I won three million dollars in the lottery this weekend, so I decided to donate a quarter of it to charity. Now I have $2,999,999.75.

707 I refused to believe my road worker father was stealing from his job, but when I got home, all the signs were there.

708 The Man Who Created Autocorrect Has Died. Restaurant in Peace.

709 I named my dog Six Miles so I can tell people that I walk six miles every single day.

710 With the rise of self-driving vehicles, it's only a matter of time before we get a country song where a guy's truck leaves him too.

711 Have hope for the future, but maybe build a bomb shelter anyway.

712 A dad is washing the car with his son.
After a moment, the son asks his father,
"Do you think we could use a sponge instead?"

713 Turning vegan is a big missed steak.

714 Son: "Dad, can you tell me what a solar eclipse is?"
Dad: "No sun."

715 I don't approve of political jokes...I've seen too many of them get elected.

716   If a child refuses to sleep during nap time, are they guilty of resisting a rest?

717   I think we should get rid of democracy. All in favor, raise your hand.

718   I gave up my seat to a blind person on the bus. That is how I lost my job as a bus driver.

719   A friend of mine tried to annoy me with bird puns, but I soon realized that toucan play at that game.

720   What's the difference between a poorly dressed man on a bicycle and a nicely dressed man on a tricycle? A tire.

721   Cleaning mirrors is a job I could really see myself doing.

722   I couldn't quite remember how to throw a boomerang, but eventually it came back to me.

723   I've just written a song about tortillas—actually, it's more of a rap.

724 My boss told me to have a good day.
So I went home.

725 My first job was working in an orange juice factory, but I got canned: I couldn't concentrate.

726 I found a rock yesterday that measured 1,760 yards in length. Must be some kind of milestone.

727 My boss is going to fire the employee with the worst posture. I have a hunch; it might be me.

728 One day you're the best thing since sliced bread. The next, you're toast.

729 There are three kinds of people: those who can count and those who can't.

730 Sorry, I just saw your text from last night— are you guys still at the restaurant?

731 People who write "u" instead of "you." What do you do with all the time you save?

732 Never ask a woman who is eating ice cream straight from the carton how she's doing.

733   My grandfather tried to warn them about the Titanic. He screamed and shouted about the iceberg and how the ship was going to sink, but all they did was throw him out of the theater.

734   My boss says I intimidate the other employees, so I just stared at him until he apologized.

735   My math teacher called me average. How mean!

736   I ordered two thousand pounds of Chinese soup. It was Won Ton.

737   The worst part about working for the department of unemployment is when you get fired, you still have to show up the next day.

738   There is a new trend in our office; everyone is naming food. I saw it today while I was eating a sandwich named Kevin.

739   A teacher asks a student, "Are you ignorant or just apathetic?" The kid answers, "I don't know and I don't care."

740 My friend claims that he "accidentally" glued himself to his autobiography, but I don't believe him. But that's his story, and he's sticking to it.

741 I wanna make a joke about sodium, but Na.

742 A bus station is where a bus stops. A train station is where a train stops. On my desk, I have a workstation.

743 I hate peer pressure and you should too.

744 Somewhere, an elderly lady reads a book on how to use the internet, while a young boy googles "how to read a book."

745 I wanna hang a map of the world in my house. Then I'm gonna put pins into all the locations that I've traveled to. But first, I'm gonna have to travel to the top two corners of the map so it won't fall down.

746 Hello, everyone, welcome to Plastic Surgery Addicts Anonymous. I see a lot of new faces here tonight.

747 Another World's Oldest Man has died.
This is beginning to look suspicious.

748 My son was like, "I got a D in math," and I was
like, "That's really bad," and my wife was like,
"You need to stop doing his homework!"

749 Where do they get the seeds to plant seedless
watermelons?

750 I ordered a chicken and an egg from Amazon.
I'll let you know.

751 I like birthdays, but I think too many can kill you.

752 Got my friend a "get better soon" card.
She's not sick, I just think she could get better.

753 I hate insect puns; they really bug me.

754 I was born to be a pessimist. My blood type is
B negative.

755 I told my niece that I saw a moose on the way
to work this morning. She said, "How do you
know he was on his way to work?"

756 I walked past a homeless guy with a sign that read, "One day, this could be you." I put my money back in my pocket, just in case he's right.

757 Can a kangaroo jump higher than the Empire State Building? Of course. The Empire State Building can't jump.

758 I am so poor I can't even pay attention.

759 I always tell new hires, don't think of me as your boss, think of me as your friend who can fire you.

760 If anything is possible, is it possible for something to be impossible?

761 I don't suffer from insanity. I enjoy every minute of it.

762 Took my dog to a bonfire, and as he sat there, staring at it blankly, I realized he loves sticks. I was burning a giant pile of his toys.

763 Brains aren't everything. In my case, they're nothing.

764   I am a nobody, nobody is perfect, therefore I am perfect.

765   The depressing thing about tennis is that no matter how good I get, I'll never be as good as a wall.

766   I just read that alligators can grow up to fifteen feet. But I haven't seen any with more than four.

767   If procrastination was an Olympic sport, I'd compete in it later.

768   What if there were no hypothetical questions?

769   When an employment application asks who is to be notified in case of emergency, I always write, "A very good doctor."

770   My wife isn't talking to me. She said I ruined her birthday. I'm not sure how. I didn't even know it was her birthday.

771   I'm reading a horror story in Braille. Something bad is about to happen...I can feel it.

772 How many of you believe in telekinesis?
Raise MY hand!

773 If we aren't supposed to eat animals, why are
they made with meat?

774 I stayed up all night wondering where the sun
went, then it dawned on me.

775 The last airline I flew charged for everything.
Except for the bad service. That was free.

776 Doesn't expecting the unexpected make the
unexpected become the expected?

777 My first child has gone off to college, and I feel
a great emptiness in my life. Specifically, in my
checking account.

778 I finally realized my parents favored my twin
brother. It hit me when they asked me to blow
up balloons for his surprise birthday party.

779 I look like a before picture.

780 If a man speaks in the forest and there is no
woman there to hear it...is he still wrong?

781 How long have I been working for this company? Ever since they threatened to fire me.

782 My neighbors are listening to great music. Whether they like it or not.

783 Whoever said nothing is impossible is a liar. I've been doing nothing for years.

784 I'm so fat, I could sell shade.

785 "I'm sorry" and "I apologize" mean the same thing...except when you're at a funeral.

786 Accidentally called 911. Set my house on fire to not look stupid.

787 Teacher: "Are you sleeping in my class?"
Student: "Well, now I'm not, but if you could be a little quieter, I could."

788 In democracy, it's your vote that counts. In feudalism, it's your count that votes.

789 Just took a power nap on a park bench. Made $7.30 in change.

790   A vegan said to me, "People who sell meat are gross!" I said, "People who sell fruits and vegetables are grocer."

791   Adam's sister, Ruth, fell off the back of his motorcycle. He just rode on. Ruthless.

792   Haikus are easy. But sometimes they don't make sense. Refrigerator.

793   How to lose an argument with a woman:
1) Argue.

794   "I ran a half marathon" sounds so much better than "I quit halfway through a marathon."

795   Education is important, but other stuff is more importanter.

796   I just got fired from my job as a taxi driver. Turns out people don't like it when you go the extra mile for them.

797   My mind wants to dance, but my body is a really awkward white guy.

798   My landlord says he needs to come talk to me about how high my heating bill is. I told him, "My door is always open."

799   As I handed my dad his fiftieth birthday card, he looked at me with tears in his eyes and said, "You know, one would have been enough."

800   All I'm saying is why blame it on being lazy when you can blame it on being old?

801   Don't mess with old people; life imprisonment is not that much of a deterrent anymore.

802   Why is "abbreviation" such a long word?

803   Why is the man who invests all your money called a broker?

804   Apparently, 29% of pet owners let their pet sleep on the bed with them, so I gave it a try. My goldfish died.

805   How do you know if someone is hitchhiking or just complimenting your driving?

806   Waitress: "Do you have any questions about the menu?" Me: "What kind of font is this?"

807   If a person told you they were a pathological liar, should you believe them?

808   I've got a phobia of over-engineered buildings. It's a complex complex complex.

809   What does "reading comprehension" even mean?

810   What do you call someone who is afraid of picnics? A basket case!

811   My boss just said to me, "You've been late five days this week...do you know what that means?" I certainly do—it's FRIDAY!

812   Evening news is where they begin with "Good evening" and then proceed to tell you why it isn't.

813   I always put in a full eight hours at work. Spread out over the course of the week.

814   I thought I was just really tired, but it's been five years, so I guess this is just how I look now.

815   Just remember, it's better to pay full price than to admit you're a senior citizen.

816   I'm here for whatever you need me to do from the couch.

817   If you put your left shoe on the wrong foot...it's on the right foot.

818   Set your Wi-Fi password to 2444666668888888. So, when someone asks for it, tell them it's 12345678.

819   I'll be doing a book signing today at Barnes & Noble from 2 p.m. until they kick me out for writing in random books.

820   My daughter told me she wants to be a secret agent. Based on that alone, I don't think she'd be a good secret agent.

821   Everybody repeat after me: "We are all individuals."

822   What do you call someone without a nose or a body? Nobodynose.

823   Do people who bring bikes on the subway realize what bikes do?

824   "How was your day, Mom?" is teenager for I-need-something-that-costs-money.

825   I love when I leave work early to surprise my wife at home and she greets me with those three very special words…"Were you fired?"

826   People say I'm condescending. That means I talk down to people.

827   Sorry I'm late. I was trying to think of ways to get out of this.

828   What happens once in a minute and twice in a moment but never in a decade? The letter M.

829   "I have a split personality," said Tom, being frank.

830   I find it very offensive when people get easily offended.

831   Remember: What dad really wants is a nap. Really.

832   When men say, "I'm fine," they actually mean it. Weirdos.

833   Dear men, "I don't want anything for my Birthday" is the same as "I'm fine." You're welcome.

834   With my luck I'll probably be reincarnated as me.

835   My wife set a limit on how much we can spend on each other for our anniversary. It's $100 on me and $500 on her.

836   I saw a chameleon today, so I guess it was a pretty lousy chameleon.

837   My wife says I only have two faults...I don't listen, and something else...

838   The three unwritten rules of life: 1. 2. 3.

839   A bus is a vehicle that runs twice as fast when you are after it as when you are in it.

840   I have kleptomania. When it gets bad, I take something for it.

841   Efficiency is a highly developed form of laziness.

842   A storm blew away 25% of my roof last night. Oof!

843   I was at a climbing center the other day, but someone had stolen all the grips from the wall; honestly, you couldn't make it up.

844   A nice Chinese couple gave me a very good camera down by the Washington Monument. I didn't really understand what they were saying, but it was very nice of them.

845   I hate it when people don't know the difference between your and you're. There so stupid.

What is black and white and red all over?

846   A newspaper.

847   A penguin falling down the stairs.

848   A communist newspaper.

849   A sunburned penguin.

850   A zebra with a rash.

851   A skunk with a diaper rash.

852   A penguin holding its breath.

853   A guy in a tuxedo without any jokes.

854   An Oreo cake with strawberries.

855   Well, simply, it's an impossibility. If one can see black and white, then it isn't red *all* over; if it *is* red all over, then one wouldn't be able to see black and white; at best, depending on the hue of the red, one might be able to discern darker and lighter shades beneath.

JOBS AND MONEY JOKES

856 I started with nothing, and I still have most of it.

857 The five signs of laziness: 1.

858 I lost my job at the bank on my first day...
a lady asked me to check her balance, so
I pushed her over.

859 Money talks. But all mine ever says is goodbye.

860 Most people are shocked when they find out
how incompetent I am as an electrician.

861 I can't believe I got fired from the calendar
factory. All I did was take a day off.

862 I just left my job—I couldn't work for my boss after what he said to me. What did he say? "You're fired!"

863 Yesterday, a passenger in a taxi cab leaned over to ask the driver a question and gently tapped him on the shoulder to get his attention. The driver screamed, lost control of the cab, nearly hit a bus, drove up over the curb, and stopped just inches from a large plate window. For a few moments everything was silent in the cab. Then, the shaking driver said, "Are you OK? I'm so sorry, but you scared the daylights out of me." The badly shaken passenger apologized to the driver and said, "I didn't realize that a mere tap on the shoulder would startle someone so badly." The driver replied, "No, no, I'm the one who is sorry, it's entirely my fault. Today is my very first day driving a cab...I've been driving a hearse for twenty-five years."

FAMILY JOKES

864 When I was a boy, I had a disease that required me to eat dirt three times a day in order to survive...it's a good thing my older brother told me about it.

865 *Children*: You spend the first two years of their life teaching them to walk and talk. Then you spend the next sixteen years telling them to sit down and be quiet.

866 A young man agreed to babysit one night so a single mother could have an evening out. At bedtime he sent the youngsters upstairs to bed and settled down to watch football. One child kept creeping down the stairs, but the young man kept sending him back to bed. At 9 p.m. the doorbell rang. It was the next-door neighbor, Mrs. Brown, asking whether her son was there. The young man brusquely replied, "No." Just then a little head appeared over the banister and shouted, "I'm here, Mom, but he won't let me go home!"

867 *Women Should Not Have Children After Thirty-Five*: I don't care what the doctor says. I don't care what your friends say. Women should not have children after thirty-five! After all, thirty-five children are enough!

868 Two kids are talking to each other. One says, "I'm really worried. My dad works twelve hours a day to give me a nice home and good food. My mom spends the whole day cleaning and cooking for me. I'm worried sick!" The other kid says, "What have you got to worry about? Sounds to me like you've got it made!" The first kid says, "What if they try to escape?"

869 One day a little girl was sitting and watching her mother do the dishes at the kitchen sink. She suddenly noticed that her mother had several strands of white hair sticking out in contrast to her brunette head. She looked at her mother and inquisitively asked, "Why are some of your hairs white, Mom?" Her mother replied, "Well, every time that you do something wrong and make me cry or feel unhappy, one of my hairs turns white." The little girl thought about this revelation for a while and then said, "Momma, how come ALL of Grandma's hairs are white?"

870 George knocked on the door of his friend's house. When his friend's mother answered, he asked, "Can Albert come out to play?" "No," said the mother, "it's too cold." "Well, then," said George, "can his football come out to play?"

871 "Is your mother home?" the salesman asked the small boy. "Yeah, she's home," the boy said, scooting over to let him pass. The salesman rang the doorbell, got no response, knocked once, then again. Still no one came to the door. Turning to the boy, the fellow said, "I thought you said your mother was home!" The kid replied, "She is, but this isn't where I live."

872 Father: I hear you skipped school to play football.
Son: No, I didn't, and I have the fish to prove it!

873 Little brother: "If you broke your arm in two places, what would you do?" Boy: "I wouldn't go back to those two places, that's for sure."

874   Little Jimmy's preschool class went on a field trip to the fire station. The firefighter giving the presentation held up a smoke detector and asked the class: "Does anyone know what this is?" Little Jimmy's hand shot up, and the firefighter called on him. Little Jimmy replied: "That's how Mommy knows supper is ready!"

875   There was a little boy named Johnny who used to hang out at the local corner market. The owner didn't know what Johnny's problem was, but the boys would constantly tease him. They would always comment that he was two bricks shy of a load, or two pickles short of a barrel. To prove it, sometimes they would offer Johnny his choice between a nickel (five cents) and a dime (ten cents), and Johnny would always take the nickel because it was bigger. One day after Johnny grabbed the nickel, the store owner took him aside and said, "Johnny, those boys are making fun of you. They think you don't know the dime is worth more than the nickel. Are you grabbing the nickel because it's bigger, or what?" Slowly, Johnny turned toward the store owner, and a big grin appeared on his face, and Johnny said, "Well, if I took the dime, they'd stop doing it, and so far, I've saved twenty dollars!"

876 What do you call a group of baby soldiers?
An infantry.

877 Parent #1: Why is there a strange baby
in the crib?
Parent #2: You told me to change the baby.

878 A baby's laugh is one of the most beautiful
things you will ever hear. Unless it is 3 a.m.,
you're home alone, and you don't have a baby.

879 Parent to her friend: I'm exhausted.
I was up with the baby until 4 a.m.
Friend: It's probably not good to keep a baby
up that late.

880 There was a dad who tried to keep his wife
happy through labor by telling jokes, but
she didn't laugh once. Know why? It was
the delivery.

881 How did the baby know she was ready to be
born? She was running out of womb.

882 Welcome to parenting. Your choices are:
A) Listen to your toddler scream and cry for ten
minutes because you opened their fruit snack.
B) Listen to your toddler scream and cry for ten

minutes because they don't know how to open their fruit snack.

883   If you open a candy wrapper in the middle of a forest with nobody around, how long until your children show up and ask what you're eating?

884   Yesterday, my four-year-old and I painted pictures, went to the park, played house, cooked dinner together, and read a long book. Or, as she described it to her teacher: "I picked up a dead bug, and Mommy yelled at me."

885   Seven-year-old: Can I have a snack?
Me: No, you'll ruin your dinner.
Seven-year-old: I thought that was your job.

886   At the drive-thru window...
Toddler: Can I say hi?
Me: Aww that's sweet. (*Rolls down window.*)
Toddler: Two milkshakes, please!

887   Why aren't you smiling in your school pictures?
Child: Because I'm at school.
Me: So?
Child: Can I see your work ID?
Me: Okay, I get it.

888   Friend: What's that thing where you're always tired but can never get rest?
Me: Parenthood.

AGING JOKES

889   Looking fifty is great...if you're sixty.

890   You know you are old when almost everything hurts, and what doesn't hurt doesn't work.

891   What goes up but never comes down? Your age!

892   Few women admit their age; few men act it.

893   I'm so old my bedtime is three hours after I fall asleep on the couch.

894   I'm so old, when I was a kid, rainbows were black and white.

895 How many old guys does it take to change a light bulb? Only one, but it might take all day.

896 She said she was approaching forty, and I couldn't help wondering from what direction.

897 Regular naps prevent old age, especially if you take them while driving.

898 You're not old until a teenager describes you as middle-aged.

899 I always feel better when my doctor says something is normal for my age, but then I realize dying will also be normal for my age at some point.

900 An old grandma brings a bus driver a bag of peanuts every day. First the bus driver enjoyed the peanuts, but after a week of eating them, he asked: "Please, granny, don't bring me peanuts anymore. Have them yourself." The granny answers: "You know, I don't have teeth anymore. I just prefer to suck the chocolate around them."

901 I'm so old I knew the Dead Sea when it was only sick.

902   By the time a man is old enough to watch his step, he's too old to go anywhere.

903   What do you call a group of rabbits hopping backwards? A receding hare-line.

904   How can you tell which rabbits are getting old? Look for the grey hares.

905   Ah, the modern days. I just saw a grandpa help a youngster who was staring into his phone to cross the street.

906   Feeling down about my thinning hair, I told a friend, "Soon I'll never need to go back to the beauty salon. Whenever I vacuum, all I pick up is my hair." A glass-half-full kind of gal, she responded, "Well, then you won't need to vacuum either."

907   We all get heavier as we get older because there's a lot more information in our heads. I'm just really intelligent, and my head couldn't hold any more, so I started filling up the rest of my body.

908   A nice thing about aging and losing your memory is you meet new friends every day.

909 A nice thing about aging is that when you lose your glasses, they're usually close by, like on your forehead.

910 Did you hear about the eighty-three-year-old woman who talked herself out of a speeding ticket by telling the young officer that she had to get to her destination before she forgot where she was going?

911 This old guy was talking to his neighbor, telling him about the new hearing aid he just got. "It cost a fortune, but it was worth it. It works perfectly." "Really," said the neighbor. "What kind is it?" "Ten-thirty."

912 I'm so old that I take a nap to get ready for bed.

913 You know you're old when you use valet parking to avoid losing your car.

914 A man has reached middle age when he is cautioned to slow down by his doctor instead of by the police.

915 You know you're getting old when you wake up exhausted from the previous night—and you didn't do anything the previous night.

916   You know you're getting old when, leaning over to pick something up off the floor, you ask yourself if there is anything else you need to do while you are down there.

917   A young man was walking through a supermarket to pick up a few things when he noticed an old lady following him around. Thinking nothing of it, he ignored her and continued on. Finally, he went to the checkout line, but she got in front of him. "Pardon me," she said, "I'm sorry if my staring at you has made you feel uncomfortable. It's just that you look just like my son, who just died recently." "I'm very sorry," replied the young man, "is there anything I can do for you?" "Yes," she said, "As I'm leaving, can you say 'Goodbye, Mother?' It would make me feel so much better." "Sure," answered the young man. As the old woman was leaving, he called out, "Goodbye, Mother!" As he stepped up to the checkout counter, he saw that his total was $127.50. "How can that be?" He asked, "I only purchased a few things!" "Your mother said that you would pay for her," said the clerk.

918   An elderly couple had dinner at another couple's house, and after eating, the wives left the table and went into the kitchen. The two gentlemen were talking, and one said, "Last night we went out to a new restaurant and it was really great. I would highly recommend it." The other man said, "What is the name of the restaurant?" The first man thought and thought and finally said, "What is the name of that flower you give to someone you love? You know…the one that's red and has thorns." "Do you mean a rose?" "Yes, that's the one," replied the man. He then turned toward the kitchen and yelled, "Rose, what's the name of that restaurant we went to last night?"

919   I think the most exciting thing about getting older is never knowing what part of your body is going to hurt the next day.

920   I'm getting so old that by the time I get up, get dressed, and have breakfast, it is 4 p.m.

921   I'm so fat and bald that bowling alleys are dangerous for me.

922   An elderly Floridian called 911 on her cell phone to report that her car had been broken into. She was hysterical as she explained her situation to the dispatcher: "They've stolen the stereo, the steering wheel, the brake pedal, and even the accelerator!" she cried. The dispatcher said, "Stay calm. An officer is on the way." A few minutes later, the officer radioed in. "Disregard," he said. "She got in the back seat by mistake."

923   The older I get, the earlier it gets late.

924   An elderly gent was invited to his old friend's home for dinner one evening. He was impressed by the way his buddy preceded every request to his wife with endearing terms—honey, my love, darling, sweetheart, pumpkin, etc. The couple had been married almost seventy years, and clearly, they were still very much in love. While the wife was in the kitchen, the man leaned over and said to his host, "I think it's wonderful that, after all these years, you still call your wife those loving pet names." The old man hung his head. "I have to tell you the truth," he said. "I forgot her name about ten years ago."

925   William's wife started noticing how forgetful he was becoming. Being the concerned wife, she convinced him to see a doctor. William was a little worried when the doctor came in. Sensing his patient's nervousness, the first thing the doctor did was to ask what was troubling him. "Well," William answered. "I seem to be getting forgetful. I'm never sure I can remember where I put the car, or whether I answered a letter, or where I'm going, or what it is I'm going to do once I get there, if I get there. So, I really need your help. What can I do?" The doctor thought for a moment, then answered in his kindest tone, "Please pay me in advance."

926 The secret of staying young is to live honestly, eat slowly, and lie about your age.

927 "How was your golf game, dear?" asked a wife. "Well, I was hitting pretty well, but my eyesight's gotten so bad I couldn't see where the ball went." "But you're seventy-five years old, Jack!" admonished his wife. "Why don't you take my brother Scott along?" "But he's eighty-five and doesn't even play golf anymore," protested Jack. "But he's got perfect eyesight. He could watch your ball," Tracy pointed out. The next day Jack teed off with Scott looking on. Jack swung, and the ball disappeared down the middle of the fairway. "Do you see it?" asked Jack. "Yup," Scott answered. "Well, where is it?" yelled Jack, peering off into the distance. "I forgot."

928 Since more and more seniors are texting, there appears to be a need for an STC (a Senior Texting Code). Please pass this on so the next generation can understand your texts.

- ATD: At The Doctor's
- BTW: Bring The Wheelchair
- BYOT: Bring Your Own Teeth
- CGU: Can't Get Up
- FWIW: Forgot Where I Was
- GGPBL: Gotta Go, Pacemaker Battery Low!
- GHA: Got Heartburn Again
- IMHAO: Is My Hearing Aid On?
- LMDO: Laughing My Dentures Out
- LOL: Living On Lipitor
- TTYL: Talk To You Louder
- WAITT: Who Am I Talking to?
- WATP: Where Are The Prunes?

929 Eventually you will reach a point when you stop lying about your age and start bragging about it.

930 How old would you be if you didn't know how old you are?

931 When you are dissatisfied and would like to go back to youth, think of algebra.

932 Perks of being old:

- Your secrets are safe with your friends because they can't remember them either.

- Your joints are more accurate meteorologists than the national weather service.
- In a hostage situation, you are likely to be released first.
- No one expects you to run—anywhere.
- People call at 9 p.m. and ask, "Did I wake you?"
- You can eat dinner at 4 p.m.
- Your eyes won't get much worse.
- You know more about prescription drugs than your pharmacist.

933   You might be old if:

- You get winded playing chess.
- Your children begin to look middle-aged.
- You know all the answers, but nobody asks the questions.
- You look forward to a dull evening.
- You sit in a rocking chair and can't get it going.
- You stop looking forward to your next birthday.
- Dialing long distance wears you out.
- Your back goes out more than you do.
- You sink your teeth into a steak and they stay there.
- The thought of getting out of bed never occurs to you.

MISCELLANEOUS

934   Pretentious? Moi?

935   What do you call cheese that isn't yours? Nacho cheese.

936   What do you get when you cross a joke with a rhetorical question?

937   Two men meet on opposite sides of a river. One shouts to the other: "I need you to help me get to the other side!" The other guy replies: "You are on the other side!"

938   I bought my friend an elephant for his room. He said, "Thanks!" I said, "Don't mention it."

939 When you look for something, why is it always in the last place you look? Because when you find it, you stop looking.

940 The only mystery in life is why the kamikaze pilots wore helmets.

941 It had been snowing for hours when an announcement came over the university's intercom: "Will the students who are parked on University Drive please move their cars so that we may begin plowing?"
Twenty minutes later there was another announcement: "Will the twelve hundred students who went to move twenty-six cars please return to class."

942 "You in the back of the room, what was the date of the signing of the Magna Carter?"
"I dunno."
"You don't? Well, let's try this. Who was Bonny Prince Charley?" "I dunno."
"Well, tell me what the Tennis Court Oath was?" "I dunno."
"I assigned this stuff last Friday. What were you doing this last weekend?" "I was out fishing with friends."
"You were? What audacity to stand there and tell me a thing like that! How do you ever

expect to pass this course?" "I don't. I just came in to fix the radiator."

943 One day a college student comes home for spring break, and he and his dad start a conversation.
"So how are your classes?" asks the father.
"Good."
"How is the football team playing this year?"
"Okay."
"Making new friends?"
"Some."
"What are you thinking of majoring in?"
"Communications."

944 Some people at a university operated a "bank" of term papers and other homework assignments where students could buy ready-made work. There were papers to suit all needs. The "bank" had A grade, B grade, and C grade papers since it would be rather suspicious if an undistinguished student suddenly handed in a brilliant essay.
A student, who had spent the weekend on pursuits other than his assignment, went to the "bank" and purchased a paper with an inconspicuous C grade. He then retyped it and handed in the work to his professor.
Soon, the student received the paper back with

the professor's comments, which read, "I wrote this paper myself twenty-five years ago, and I always thought it should have been graded an A, so now I'm more than pleased to give it one!"

945 College student: Hey, Dad—I've got some great news for you!
Father: What, son?
College student: Remember that $500 you promised me if I made the Dean's list?
Father: I certainly do.
College student: Well, you get to keep it!

946 I have an inferiority complex, but it's not a very good one.

947 How many graduate students does it take to change a lightbulb?
Only one, but it may take them more than five years to do it.

948 In college, I was so broke I couldn't pay the electricity bill.
Those were the darkest days of my life.

949 Two wrongs don't make a right...
but three lefts do.

950   Kleptomaniacs take things literally.

951   My grandfather always said, "Don't watch your money, watch your health." So, one day while I was watching my health, someone stole my money. It was my grandfather.

952   I just found out I'm colorblind. The diagnosis came completely out of the purple.

953   Unless your name is Google, stop acting like you know everything.

954   People in the UK eat more bananas than monkeys. Last year they consumed 82,198,695 bananas and only four monkeys!

955   A recent scientific study showed that out of 2,293,618,367 people, 94% are too lazy to actually read that number.

956   Did you hear about the two psychiatrists who passed each other on a walk? One said to the other, "You're fine, how am I?"

957   A man got hit hard in the head with a can of 7Up. He's alright, though, it was a soft drink.

958 What is the definition of an optimist?
A college student who opens his wallet and expects to find money.

959 Support bacteria—they're the only culture some people have.

960 Teacher: Didn't I tell you to stand at the end of the line?
Student: I tried, but there was someone already there!

961 Two parents were talking one day and asked the other what their son was taking in college. The one replied, "He's taking every penny I have!"

962 Teacher: If I had six oranges in one hand and seven apples in the other, what would I have?
Student: Big hands!

963 Teacher: If you got twenty dollars from five people, what would you get?
Student: A new bike.

964 Teacher: What is the shortest month?
Student: May, it only has three letters.

965   A student comes back to the dorm and finds his roommate near tears.
"What's the matter, pal?" he asked.
"I wrote home for my parents to send money so that I could buy a laptop, and they sent me the laptop," he moaned.

966   "Class, do you know how many hours you are wasting on your smart phones daily?" A quiet hush falls over the class. One student breaks it up: "I know, sir, let's google it!"

967   An out-of-towner drove his car into a ditch in a desolated area. Luckily, a local farmer came to help with his big strong horse named Buddy. He hitched Buddy up to the car and yelled, "Pull, Nellie, pull!" Buddy didn't move. Then the farmer hollered, "Pull, Buster, pull!" Buddy didn't respond. Once more the farmer commanded, "Pull, Coco, pull!" Nothing. Then the farmer nonchalantly said, "Pull, Buddy, pull!" And the horse easily dragged the car out of the ditch. The motorist was most appreciative and very curious. He asked the farmer why he called his horse by the wrong name three times. The farmer said, "Oh, Buddy is blind, and if he thought he was the only one pulling, he wouldn't even try!"

968 A man buys a parrot and brings him home. But the parrot starts insulting him and gets really nasty, so the man picks up the parrot and tosses him into the freezer to teach him a lesson. He hears the bird squawking for a few minutes, but all of a sudden, the parrot is quiet. The man opens the freezer door, and the parrot walks out, looks up at him, and says, "I apologize for offending you, and I humbly ask your forgiveness." The man says, "Well, thank you. I forgive you." The parrot then says, "If you don't mind my asking, what did the chicken do?"

969 A woman brought a very limp duck into a veterinary surgeon. As she laid her pet on the table, the vet pulled out his stethoscope and listened to the bird's chest. After a moment or two, the vet shook his head and sadly said, "I'm sorry, your duck, Cuddles, has passed away." The distressed woman wailed, "Are you sure?" "Yes, I am sure. Your duck is dead," replied the vet. "How can you be so sure?" she protested. "I mean, you haven't done any testing on him or anything. He might just be in a coma or something." The vet rolled his eyes, turned around, and left the room. He returned a few minutes later with a black Labrador Retriever. As the duck's owner looked on in amazement, the dog stood on his hind legs, put his front paws on the examination table, and sniffed the duck from top to bottom. He then looked up at the vet with sad eyes and shook his head. The vet patted the dog on the head and took it out of the room. A few minutes later, he returned with a cat. The cat jumped on the table and also delicately sniffed the bird from head to foot. The cat sat back on its haunches, shook its head, meowed softly, and strolled out of the room. The vet looked at the woman and said, "I'm sorry, but as I said, this is most definitely, 100% certifiably, a dead duck." The vet turned to his computer terminal, hit a few keys, and produced a bill, which he handed to the woman. The duck's owner, still in shock, took the bill. "$150!" she cried. "$150 just to tell me my duck is dead!" The vet shrugged. "I'm sorry. If you had just taken my word for it, the bill would have been $20, but with the lab report and the cat scan, it's now $150."

970 Someone threw cheese at me. Real mature.

971 A new type of broom has come out. It is sweeping the nation.

972 I am going bananas. That's what I say to my bananas before I leave the house.

973   I have branches, but no fruit, trunk, or leaves. What am I? A bank.

974   The more of this there is, the less you see. What is it? Darkness.

WISH THEY HADN'T SAID THAT...

975 "Computers in the future may weigh no more than 1.5 tons."
Popular Mechanics, forecasting the relentless march of science, 1949.

976 "I have traveled the length and breadth of this country and talked with the best people, and I can assure you that data processing is a fad that won't last out the year."
The editor in charge of business books for Prentice Hall, 1957.

977 "But what...is it good for?"
Engineer at the Advanced Computing Systems Division of IBM, 1968, commenting on the microchip.

978 "This 'telephone' has too many shortcomings to be seriously considered as a means of communication. The device is inherently of no value to us."
Western Union internal memo, 1876.

979 "The wireless music box has no imaginable commercial value. Who would pay for a message sent to nobody in particular?"
David Sarnoff's associates in response to his urgings for investment in the radio in the 1920s.

980 "The concept is interesting and well-formed, but in order to earn better than a 'C,' the idea must be feasible."
A Yale University management professor in response to Fred Smith's paper proposing reliable overnight delivery service (which became FedEx).

981 "I don't know what use anyone could find for a machine that would make copies of documents. It certainly couldn't be a feasible business by itself."
The head of IBM, refusing to back the idea, forcing the inventor to found Xerox.

982   "Heavier-than-air flying machines are impossible."
Lord Kelvin, president, Royal Society, 1895.

983   "If I had thought about it, I wouldn't have done the experiment. The literature was full of examples that said you can't do this."
Spencer Silver on the work that led to the unique adhesives for 3M Post-It notepads.

984   "So, we went to Atari and said, 'Hey, we've got this amazing thing, even built with some of your parts, and what do you think about funding us? Or we'll give it to you. We just want to do it. Pay our salary, we'll come work for you.' And they said, 'No.' So then we went to Hewlett-Packard, and they said, 'Hey, we don't need you. You haven't got through college yet.'"
Apple Computer Inc. founder Steve Jobs on attempts to get Atari and HP interested in his and Steve Wozniak's personal computer.

985   "Professor Goddard does not know the relation between action and reaction and the need to have something better than a vacuum against which to react. He seems to lack the basic knowledge ladled out daily in high schools."
1921 New York Times editorial about Robert Goddard's revolutionary rocket work.

986 "Stocks have reached what looks like a permanently high plateau."
Irving Fisher, Professor of Economics, Yale University, 1929.

987 "Airplanes are interesting toys but of no military value."
Marechal Ferdinand Foch, Professor of Strategy, Ecole Superieure de Guerre.

988 "Everything that can be invented has been invented."
Charles H. Duell, Commissioner, U.S. Office of Patents, 1899.

989 "Louis Pasteur's theory of germs is ridiculous fiction."
Pierre Pachet, Professor of Physiology at Toulouse, 1872.

990 "The abdomen, the chest, and the brain will forever be shut from the intrusion of the wise and humane surgeon."
Sir John Eric Ericksen, British surgeon, appointed Surgeon- Extraordinare to Queen Victoria 1873.

991 "640K ought to be enough for anybody."
Bill Gates, 1981.

992 "Man will never reach the moon regardless of all future scientific advances."
Dr. Lee DeForest, father of radio and grandfather of television.

993 "The bomb will never go off. I speak as an expert in explosives."
Admiral William Leahy, US Atomic Bomb Project.

994 "There is no likelihood man can ever tap the power of the atom."
Robert Millikan, Nobel Prize in Physics, 1923.

995 "A cookie store is a bad idea. Besides, the market research reports say America likes crispy cookies, not soft and chewy cookies like you make."
Response to Debbi Fields' idea of starting Mrs. Fields' Cookies.

996 "The supercomputer is technologically impossible. It would take all of the water that flows over Niagara Falls to cool the heat generated by the number of vacuum tubes required."
Professor of Electrical Engineering, New York University.

997 "Who...would want to read a book about a bunch of crazy Swedes on a raft?"
Editor, turning down The Kon Tiki Expedition.

998 "We don't like their sound, and guitar music is on the way out,"
Decca Recording Co., rejecting the Beatles, 1962.

999 "Drill for oil? You mean drill into the ground to try and find oil? You're crazy."
Drillers whom Edwin L. Drake tried to enlist to his project to drill for oil in 1859.

1000 "There is no reason anyone would want a computer in their home."
Ken Olson, president, chairman and founder of Digital Equipment Corp., 1977.

1001 "I think there is a world market for maybe five computers."
Thomas Watson, chairman of IBM, 1943.